Ancient Greece in Film and Popular Culture

Why are so few films set in ancient Greece? And why are people so mean about the ones that are?

"Film taps into and reinforces popular ideas about the ancient world. Time and again, it chooses Rome over Greece, or dresses up Greek stories as Roman ones. Hollywood has a problem with Greece; why? This book suggests that Hollywood's problem is part of a larger set of anxieties of reception; that it reflects a basic uncertainty about how to put the idea of Greekness to work. 'Greece' matters, but it also gives people headaches."

In this accessible book, Nisbet makes sense of *Troy*, *Alexander* and *300* against the diversity of classical pasts offered by popular media including TV, comics and the Internet. He argues for a fresh approach to the ancient world on film, and to classical reception studies.

Gideon Nisbet is Lecturer in Classics at the University of Birmingham. He is the author of *Greek Epigram in the Roman Empire: Martial's Forgotten Rivals*, and appeared in the BBC4 documentary *Mary Renault: Love and War in Ancient Greece*.

REVIEWS OF THE FIRST EDITION

'... the time is ripe for turning scholarly (and student) attention to what Greece means in modern popular culture (and why). Gideon Nisbet's book, part of Bristol Phoenix Press's *Greece and Rome Live* series, serves as a brief but punchy account of the topic, and will be of considerable value to a wide audience.

'... A distinctive contribution to recent debates in reception studies [by] someone who knows what it is to receive and respond to the ancient past.'

Bryn Mawr Classical Review

'Nisbet's volume is a thoughtful and thought-provoking work on the issues of reception that I foresee becoming a standard text for both students and scholars of classics and film.'

Intertexts

'...draws on a range of popular media, including film, TV and comics, to explore and expose the preconceptions that have for so long dictated the mise-en-scène of our imaginations.'

The Anglo-Hellenic Review

A companion volume, *Ancient Rome at the Cinema: Story and Spectacle in Hollywood and Rome,* by Elena Theodorakopoulos will be published by Bristol Phoenix Press in 2009.

Ancient Greece

in

Film and Popular Culture

Updated Second Edition

Gideon Nisbet

BRISTOL
PHOENIX
PRESS

Cover illustration: from *The Colossus of Rhodes*

First published in 2006 by
Bristol Phoenix Press
an imprint of The Exeter Press
Reed Hall, Streatham Drive
Exeter, Devon EX4 4QR
UK

Updated second edition published 2008

www.exeterpress.co.uk

© Gideon Nisbet 2006; new material, 2008

The right of Gideon Nisbet to be identified
as author of this work has been asserted by him
in accordance with the Copyright, Designs and Patents Act 1988

Every effort has been made to contact copyright holders in order to obtain
permission for use of the illustrations. We would like to take this opportunity to
acknowledge any copyright holder that we may have failed to contact.

British Library Cataloguing in Publication Data
A catalogue record for this book is available from the British Library

Paperback ISBN 13: 978 1 904675 78 5

Typeset by Carnegie Book Production, Lancaster in Chaparral Pro 11pt on 15pt
Printed in Great Britain by Antony Rowe, Chippenham

CONTENTS

ILLUSTRATIONS

Preface

The Dog in the Night-time

Greece, around the beginning of the fourth century BC: Thucydides, an exiled Athenian general turned historian (one of the Western world's first), throws together a thought experiment to showcase his new-and-improved methodologies:

> I reckon that if Sparta were to become a ghost town – if just its temples, and the ruins of its public buildings, survived – then people in the future would have a hard time squaring the legend of 'Sparta' with its real power. As it is, the Spartans occupy two-fifths of the Peloponnese and exercise leadership over the whole peninsula. They also have plenty of allies outside it. But their city lacks definition and identity; it has no fine temples or grand municipal buildings. Instead, it's an old-fashioned string of villages – hardly likely to impress those visitors of the future. Athens, on the other hand – if Athens were to end up similarly deserted, I imagine that the visual impact of her ruins would persuade visitors that she had been twice as powerful as she actually was.
>
> Thucydides, *History of the Peloponnesian War* 1

Thucydides was uncanny in his prediction, as spot-on as Plato's vision of cinema (see ch.1). His future – which is to say, our present and past – has panned out pretty much exactly as he imagined.

For tourists, revolutionaries, antiquarians and patriots, Greece has meant Athens. We look at the city's picturesque ruins – above all, at the Acropolis and its landmark temple of Athena, the Parthenon – and project our own nostalgia backwards in time, attaching to a select few blocks of marble 'the glory that was Greece'. The 'we' of that last sentence is, of course, implicitly selective, entailing (at least) enough of an education to make us susceptible to the Parthenon's raddled allure. Receptions of ancient Greece are not only strongly differentiated by social class; they also help articulate status, often aspirationally. In fact, this process was under way as long ago as the Roman Empire, when Athens, then a pretty university town, traded on its past glories of philosophy and literature (Thucydides included) to charm and overcharge socially ambitious Roman tourists hungry for old-world culture. Today, the equation of Athens with classical Greece is, on the face of it, more diverse; it reproduces itself at all levels of culture, by way of tourist souvenirs as much as university syllabuses.

As we will see, though, older and more exclusive meanings are never far beneath the surface. Thucydides' rhetoric would apply just as well to modern **receptions** of the ancient world – and in particular to its representations in film, where, like Sparta to Athens, Greece has always existed in Rome's shadow. The recent blockbusters, *Troy* and *Alexander*, are anomalies in their attempt to make Greece the star – and even they find ways to keep it more or less out of the picture (see chs.2 and 3). Cinema's Greece, like the Sparta of Thucydides, has lingered as a pale ghost at the fringes of popular consciousness. Even Athens, Thucydides' star attraction, is instantly eclipsed by the trumpet blast and primary Technicolor of 'Rome'. (It's worth noting in passing that these recent blockbusters give Athens a wide berth; we'll look into some of the possible reasons for this along the way.) *Ancient Greece in Film and Popular Culture* is a short book, like all the *Greece and Rome Live!* series;

but cast around in your memory for Hellenic heroes on screen and you might wonder whether there's enough material even to fill a pamphlet. To a degree, Greece's obscurity is self-perpetuating: studios don't make movies about Greece because studios don't make movies about Greece (because ...); and this is a cycle seemed unlikely to break, given their staggering expense and disappointing reception. I'd argue – and 300 now confirms – that there's more to the story than this.

'Is there any point to which you would wish to draw my attention?'
'To the curious incident of the dog in the night-time.'
'The dog did nothing in the night-time.'
'That was the curious incident,' remarked Sherlock Holmes.
Arthur Conan Doyle, 'The Adventure of Silver Blaze',
from *The Memoirs of Sherlock Holmes*

Like Holmes' dog in the night, ancient Greece's failure to make a noise in popular culture *means* something – both about popular culture, and about what 'Greece' means to us today.

My first and longest chapter, 'Socrates' Excellent Adventure', explores some possible explanations for the failure of 'Greece' – the land, its history, its myths – as a viable subject for cinema. Why is Rome so much more attractive than Greece to film-makers, so much easier to sell to cinema audiences? The chapter begins with Socrates in the cult comedy *Bill and Ted's Excellent Adventure* (1989), escaping from Greece into good cinema. It goes on to consider three brave but ultimately unsuccessful attempts to put Greece on film, by three well-known and talented directors who never made the mistake again: Roger Corman's *Atlas* (1960), Sergio Leone's *The Colossus of Rhodes* (1961), and Robert Wise's *Helen of Troy* (1956). Critics have not been kind to these films; *Atlas* and *Colossus* in particular have been subjected to ridicule, written off as trashy and inept **pepla** (a term we might want to try and reclaim). These films conform to (and thus reinforce) our prejudices about the poor cinematic value of films set in ancient Greece – or at least they have been represented as conforming to them. But how did this set of prejudices evolve? And, given their presence, did films like these ever have a chance?

Ch.2, 'Mythconceptions', begins by exploring the representations of the only hero from Greek myth to have kept his instant brand-name recognition. Hercules (Herakles to the Greeks – as if popular culture cares) is the only successful ancient Greek cinematic franchise. The subject of countless sword-and-sandal flicks – and latterly a major TV star – he is probably as famous now as he ever was. That success has come at a price. The Hercules industry has gone hand in hand with a consistent downplaying of other themes from Greek myth; often it has swallowed other myths whole. And parts of Hercules' own story remain too dangerous to tell. Does this leave *any* options open for Greek heroism on screen? Perhaps not, if the indifferent critical and popular response to *Troy* is anything to go by; but we need to turn to representations in other popular media to understand why this response took the form it did.

Ch.3, 'Wars of the Successors', aims to do for history what ch.2 does for myth, and *Alexander* obviously looms large. The internet war of rumours between rival Alexander projects – is Alexander gay, is he a Greek, what kind of face fits? – brought modern tensions into the open; clearly, 'Greece' and Greekness continue to be as much a can of worms as they ever were. Hollywood spin suggests some useful ways of thinking about Alexander's own myth-making; and perhaps even about the race to create the 'sequel' to classical Greece and Alexander that historians call the **Hellenistic** Age. More importantly, it reminds us that reception never resolves itself or offers up a final answer. If we want comfortable certainties we can always go back to that old chestnut, the 'Classical Tradition'; but the *Alex-*

ander fracas in particular might encourage us to stick with reception if only to see where it will take us next. Ch. 4, 'It's Raining Men' (new to this edition), dines in heck with 300 and finds that ancient Greece continues to live – via reception – in interesting times.

As its title stresses, the aim of this book is to explore receptions of Greece in modern *popular* culture. I have chosen to limit the discussion primarily to films made or distributed in English (including dubbed versions), with some other popular media in a supporting role; but it is worth acknowledging from the outset that this book could have been much more diverse but for considerations of length. To a degree, the final cut reflects not just my own experiences as a filmgoer but also my participation in particular **subcultures**; even here, though, there is much less included than there could have been on (for instance) comics and science fiction. (Receptions of Greece and Rome in these alternative media would be worth a book in themselves.) The emphasis will also be too squarely Western for some tastes. There is much I could have said, for instance, about the uses Japanese popular culture makes of Greek antiquity – especially in *manga*, the Japanese equivalent to comics and graphic novels. What films to choose, though? *Troy* and *Alexander* were givens; but I decided early on in the project to avoid concentrating too much on the acknowledged classics of the genre; there is little here, for instance, on *300 Spartans* (1962) or the Kirk Douglas *Ulysses* (1955). Instead I have consciously weighted my narrative in favour of fun, out-of-the-way examples that not everyone will have seen. My agenda here is not nerdish one-upmanship, although that is a risk that a book like this must always run, especially when written by a classicist and sci-fi fan. (Reverence for the obscure is a defining trait of both subcultures.) Instead my emphasis on decided non-'classics' reflects two related but distinct preoccupations. Firstly, in common with many cultural studies practitioners, my underlying conviction is that 'X' does not mark the spot – but that a thousand small 'x's map out a cultural field pretty effectively. Towering, one-of-a-kind masterpieces may be appropriate receptacles for awe but, as symptoms and indicators of popular culture's nitty-gritty, they are rather less useful than the sequels, knock-offs, makings-of and straight-to-video cash-ins that so greatly outnumber them. More revealing again is the way that audiences and interest groups engage with these run-of-the-mill receptions and make them their own; indeed, this is one of the book's recurring themes. Secondly, I was concerned to avoid instating yet another cut-and-dried Western Canon (or Canon Lite). The great promise of reception studies to the academic discipline of classical studies in the 1990s was that we would kick our knee-jerk Great Books habit overnight, junk the tired old 'classics vs. trash' divide and get stuck into some proper cultural studies, defining 'culture' broadly, diversely and with a conspicuously small 'c'. Things never quite panned out that way on the ground; classics-and-film courses sprang up everywhere, but quickly set up a supplementary and ersatz canon of Roman screen 'classics', all safely contained by a long-ago golden age of film (*Ben-Hur*, *Quo Vadis* ...), with big-name stars and genius directors (Charlton Heston, Stanley Kubrick ...) seamlessly swapped in as substitute Dead White European Males. To avoid making this backward step a second time with receptions of Greece, I emphasise the need to embrace and engage with a consciously diverse model of reception right from the start – trash and all. It helps that the 'trash' is often more overtly about fun anyway; I was also concerned to limit the book to films that a mainstream audience might watch and get a kick out of. Readers will find nothing here, then, on the Italian and Greek attempts at filming Greek tragedy, interesting and intelligent though those films often are. Mainstream British and American cinema audiences are generally allergic to subtitles, writing off films such as

Cacoyannis' *Iphigenia* (1977) or Pasolini's *Medea* (1970) as boring art-house elitism.

Of course, the reason why they are so often dismissed that way – and often sight unseen – is one more instance of the peculiar place that 'Greece' occupies in the Western popular imagination. The West has played a centuries-long game of compare-and-contrast between ancient and modern Greece, typically with preconceived answers in mind, and in a different or indeed a longer book this might merit a chapter of its own. Still, the questions that interest me are questions of culture. I treat films (and other media texts) not as self-sufficient and inviolate 'great works', but as cultural products. Films are the raw materials of an often strongly participatory popular culture, which responds to them actively as well as passively consuming them. How 'good' a film is takes a strict second place. It is important to a work of this kind to retain an element of critical appraisal, not just because it is such fun to do, but also by way of acknowledging what is sometimes called 'positionality'. In popular culture, we are all embedded observers; one point I shall keep trying to make is that we might as well acknowledge not just the impossibility but also the undesirability of maintaining (a pretence of) academic distance from material of this kind. All the same, pointed criticism in a personal voice need not turn into **auteurist** connoisseurship. What a film-maker might have 'intended' is, for me at least, neither here nor there. Instead, I want to know what culture's consumers (who are also to some degree its producers) make of it all; the (often surprising) uses they put these products to; and the ways they fit them into their experience of the world. This emphasis also influences my resolutely eclectic choice of illustrations. As with the films, I steer away from the predictable icons, the Brad Pitts and Orlando Blooms. Instead, I head for those thousand small 'x's of subculture and audience response via ephemera and comics (ancient and modern).

Film taps into, and reinforces, popular ideas about the ancient world. Time and again, it chooses Rome over Greece, or dresses up Greek stories as Roman ones. Hollywood has a problem with Greece; why? This book suggests that Hollywood's problem is part of a larger set of anxieties of reception; that it reflects a basic uncertainty about how to put the idea of Greekness to work. 'Greece' matters; but it also gives people headaches. Our struggle to come to terms with it is always inconclusive. If the answers were easier, if they left us feeling satisfied, then Greece would be in a lot more movies; but then Greekness wouldn't continue to matter as much as it clearly does.

ACKNOWLEDGEMENTS

I am indebted to students at Reading, Warwick, Birmingham and Glasgow, and to friends in the comics and sci-fi communities, for humouring and even sharing my enthusiasms. Among friends and colleagues in Birmingham, Elena Theodorakopoulos (herself a formidable expert on ancient Rome in film) steered me towards The Exeter Press; Diana Spencer critiqued early drafts, helped compile the index and set me right on the Alexander myth, then and now. The two anonymous readers of the first submitted draft, and Vicky Stevens, the book's copy-editor, made many positive suggestions for improvement. For kind permission to reproduce images I thank David Holliday of Wetherspoon's and particularly Eric Shanower, *Age of Bronze* writer-artist, who was enthusiastic for the project and helpfully supplied images in digital format. Anna Henderson saw the book to completion at The Exeter Press – twice, now, with the Second Edition which she has rashly encouraged. May it rain men for her. Finally, my publisher and editor, John Betts, supported the project from the start; his input and commitment were invaluable throughout. The first edition of this book was affectionately dedicated to him; the second mourns his passing. 'Shadows and dust ...'.

A Note on
Terminology

I have generally avoided technical language, but some terminology is too useful to be left out (or too tedious to paraphrase). Specialist terms, or everyday words used in a specialised sense, are highlighted in **bold** on their first appearance in the main text. An alphabetical glossary of these terms is at the end of the book (pp.157–63). Like everything else here, its 'definitions' are written to provoke discussion, and reflect my own work and life interests.

1

SOCRATES' EXCELLENT
ADVENTURE

We sit in the cavernous dark. We are spectators; from an unseen point behind us, projected light throws flickering images onto the wall before our eyes. We jump at shadows, thrill at empty shapes. Where are we?

Most obviously to a modern audience we are in a cinema, watching a film. For the *cognoscenti*, whether classicists or film critics, we are somewhere else at the same time – in Plato's Cave, one of the most famous allegories or thought-experiments in the history of ideas.

Over the century or so since the invention of cinema, the Cave has become a cliché of film criticism – understandably so, as the parallels are obvious and close. Struck by the cute similarities of the Cave to a modern cinema, critics have leaned upon Plato's account of the limitations of the physical senses to prop up their own rhetorical flights of fancy. Like the Cave, the cinema has been characterised as a simulacrum, a lie about reality; and as a mechanism constructed to draw out the lower passions (or the passions of the lower orders). This interest has translated into renewed fame for the Cave itself – at least within the groves of academe. Today, ironically, more people have probably heard of Plato's allegory via books and courses on film theory than by reading his *Republic* as philosophy or literature.

I say 'ironically' because Plato would have hated cinema. Certainly he would have insisted on banning it from his ideal society as outlined in *The Republic*, the context in which the allegory of the Cave is originally introduced. Plato brings us into the Cave in Book 7 of *The Republic* with the specific aim of proving that the impressions we receive via our senses are unreliable, that they do not deserve our serious attention. To be sure, Plato's suspicion of sensation, his contempt for crowd-pleasing spectacle, have met with some admirers at the more elitist end of film criticism; yet it would be hard to think of anyone more implacably hostile to the moving image.

Plato's allegory of the Cave raises additional difficulties when we turn to movies about ancient Greece – its histories, its heroes, its myths. One problem (and by no means a trivial one) is that self-righteous eggheads like Plato still dominate popular culture's idea of 'Greece', thus limiting the stories that cinema can tell about it. (At times the presence of a philosopher seems almost obligatory; but what can you make him do for the camera?) This is part of a broader problem. Viewed as a thought-experiment, the Cave may still dazzle the dons with its flashy ontological riffs; but it is a bad cinema and its attractions are boring. From the point of view of a demanding modern audience, Plato's prototype cinema-goers, goggling uncritically at the flickering shadows of everyday objects, are much too easily pleased. Plato's hostility to visual pleasure is by the by; probably very few of his contemporaries knew or cared about his bizarre theories. Instead, the question is: how can their world – the world of Plato and his contemporaries – translate into good cinema?

Greece as Anti-Cinema

I begin not with one of the few – very few – obvious movie texts but with a 1980s California teen-buddy movie, *Bill and Ted's Excellent Adventure* (1989). The plot is the time-travelling interventionism of *The Terminator* played for laughs. (There are echoes, too, of the successful *Back to the Future* franchise.) Bill S. Preston 'Esq.' and Ted 'Theodore' Logan, two perpetually flunking high school students, must get an 'A' for their history presentation or fail the course. Unknown to the two of them, future civilisation in all its camp and bouffant glory is depending on their success. A mentor from the future is sent back with a time machine to help them collect raw material for their presentation. Set the task of describing how a range of historical characters would have viewed their tacky California hometown of San Dinas in the late twentieth century, the boys go about the problem in the most direct way imaginable, shoplifting famous historical 'dead dudes' and transporting them to the present day via a Pacific Bell telephone box (in a nice tip of the hat to the BBC classic *Doctor Who*). An early acquisition is the ancient Athenian philosopher 'So-crates' (two syllables, rhymes with 'mates').

The boys arrive in ancient Athens in company with their first acquisition, Billy the Kid. The party has narrowly escaped being gunned down in an exciting brawl / chase sequence in Billy's noisy and colourful Wild West; the contrast between the two scenes could not be more stark. At the level of **mise-en-scène**, Athens consists of rocks, dust, unconvincing colonnades and scraggy topiary. Worse, there is an educational caption: 'Athens, Greece. 410 BC'. This sets alarm bells ringing; can subtitles be far away?

The film-makers immediately set the scene – and the mood – via static, lingering establishing shots: white marble statues of bearded sages, in head-and-shoulders close-up, and a featureless stone wall. Athens is thus established from the start, via **cinematography**, as the polar opposite of cinema's ancient Rome. Roman films typically open with a grandiose, panoramic long shot. A good example is *The Robe* (1953), the first movie to be released in the widescreen CinemaScope format; its opening sequence uses panning to add further emphasis to the sweeping scope of the spectacle on offer. By way of contrast, the Athens of *Bill and Ted* is characterized throughout by static close-ups and medium shots which confine our field of view. Each shot is held for at least a second too long; it sounds very little but it stands in strong opposition to the snappy pacing and quick editing of the rest of the movie.

A static medium shot shows us two elderly, robed men (seen from behind) walking slowly up a set of steps towards an incomprehensible male speaker (not seen). Thus far, Athens is not a good movie. The camera then pans down and left to introduce Bill and Ted – the first use of movement in the scene. The boys are tanned and colourfully dressed in orange and a lilac print, establishing a strong visual contrast to the dull natural colours of Athenian costuming. In terms both of cinematography and of mise-en-scène, they are not at home here.

Leaving Billy the Kid – who is already clearly bored by Athens – to mind the phone booth, Bill and Ted locate 'So-crates' on what we must take to be the Acropolis. We cut to a medium shot of a bearded, white-clad Socrates lecturing a politely bored audience of seated, robed men, whose mood is signalled by facial expression and body language, two further aspects of mise-en-scène. Socrates gestures stiffly, and speaks – incomprehensibly. Accompanying his lecture comes the cinematic kiss of death for foreign-language films at the box office, subtitling:

> So you see – our lives are just specks of dust falling through the fingers of time.

This shot lasts 11 seconds; it seems an eternity. Then camera movement (panning) is used once more, again to bring Bill and Ted into scene. In strong contrast to Socrates' reserved and stilted body language, theirs is open and relaxed. Socrates is quickly wooed with improvised philosophy, worked up out of heavy metal lyrics ('all

1. 'Party on, dude' (*Bill and Ted's Excellent Adventure*):
So-crates gets his *Ben-Hur* moment.

we are is dust in the wind, dude'). Instantly, he becomes open and animated, gesticulating and laughing enthusiastically. He will keep this new body language – really a new persona – in his subsequent adventures across time.

If anything, Socrates' conversion to the cause of helping two twentieth-century slackers get their homework done is suspiciously hasty and wholehearted. Perhaps he can already smell the hemlock (an ultimate fate of which academic under-achievers Bill and Ted naturally remain oblivious); but I think there's more to it than that. Throughout the movie, 'So-crates' will be visibly and touchingly grateful for this once-in-a-lifetime opportunity *not* to be in a film about Ancient Greece.

It is striking how quickly and how thoroughly he enters into the anarchic spirit of the movie; and, most of all, how he embraces the chance to have exciting adventures – a chance that a Greek movie would never allow to a typecast bearded philosopher. Most of all, a Greek movie would frustrate Socrates in his (heretofore closeted)

urge to show off, to be a consumer and producer of visual pleasure
– to play to the crowd. (His showmanship in the Beethoven kidnap
is a joy to behold.) Joining an oddball assortment of famous person-
ages on a trans-historical looting spree – action! sports! romance!
– is the antithesis of the dialogue-heavy typecasting to which
cinematic Greece had condemned him.

In fact, if Socrates is in any genre during *Bill and Ted* – teen /
buddy comedy excepted – it is, surprisingly, that of the *Roman*
movie. Cackling with glee, Socrates teams up with Billy the Kid to
rescue the boys from a mediaeval castle in a high-speed wagon chase
– at last, a chance to play charioteer! (Fig. 1) Socrates has changed
horses in mid-race, abandoning an unsuccessful genre for a productive and vibrant idiom. Rome has triumphed over Greece.

This may seem an odd statement in the early years of the third
millennium, surrounded as we now are by a rash of Greek-themed
film projects – for all that many of them are busy going nowhere. In
the wake of the Roman box-office smash *Gladiator* (2000), famous-
name directors fell over themselves to develop new treatments of
previously filmed stories from antiquity. Sidestepping the time-
worn pieties of Hollywood's classic Roman narratives, they turned
to Greek myth and history for their inspiration: the ten-year siege
of Troy, the campaigns of Alexander the Great, the self-sacrifice of
the 300 Spartans at Thermopylae. On television, Hercules was still
cleaning up in the re-runs (with the help of his quasi-Amazon buddy
Xena). Are announcements of the death of the *peplum* premature?
We'll have to wait and see; so far, and 300 aside, the omens are not
good, for cinema at least. (I shall have much more to say about *Troy*
and the rival *Alexander* projects in chs.2 and 3.) In the meantime,
we can try to pin down the factors that made so many film-makers
and fans *want* to see it dead.

Greece at the Drive-In

One obvious reason for the relative scarcity of Hollywood films set in ancient Greece is the difficulty of selling Greece to cinema audiences. As Thucydides pointed out (in the same up-front methodology primer as his Athens-vs-Sparta scenario), Greece's physical and political geography are inconveniently fiddly – dozens of islands, several distinct ethnicities, hundreds of independent and frequently warring city-based states. Its history is correspondingly complicated and its politics even worse. An empire like Rome's seems (misleadingly) easy to get a handle on – but a mess of bickering city-states, followed by a half-dozen warring kingdoms? Even university students often have a hard time remembering who's who. For a mainstream audience this is too much like hard work. In any case, what's in it for them? Canny film-makers have to find ways of pitching the idea of Greece in ways that coincide with an audience's idea of a good time.

To do so, they must overcome or sidestep some major shortcomings. *Bill and Ted* highlights a crucial problem: audiences assume Greece is boring (or 'intellectual', which amounts to the same thing for a mainstream cinema audience weaned on pervasive anti-intellectualism). Greece is also morally dubious (again, see 'intellectual') – but without the enticing eye-candy of Roman vices. No orgies, gladiators, and dancing girls; instead, popular preconceptions of Greek private life circle obsessively around the Hollywood hot potato of male same-sex desire, still sometimes sniggeringly referred to as 'Greek love'. This essentially Victorian reception continues to compromise all of classical Greece's modern pop-culture receptions; we shall examine its origin shortly but its lurking presence will be a recurring theme throughout the book. Rome, on the other hand, is very Hollywood – far easier to package for audiences. Whether or not we have been there, or know much about its history, we feel we know Rome already; we feel at home in Roman movies because they reflect the furniture of our everyday urban experiences. Roman presences – some obvious, others more subtle – pervade our built environments, from town halls to shopping centres. Thucydides' prediction of Athens as a sure-fire future crowd-puller is true only to the limited extent that it still has a place on the see-before-you-die lists of conscientious site-seers; it's Rome that is iconic. Of course, half of what we consider 'Roman' is Greek to begin with – Corinthian columns, pedimented gables – but this only confirms the primacy of Roman style as the ultimate in successful appropriations, inviting us in turn to imitate it ourselves. Rome is such a superlative recycler of Greek motifs that the originals are themselves easily taken for poor copies. This is a difficulty we shall see recurring in movies that try to evoke a visual image of ancient Greece; what can it *look like*, if not a pale imitation of movies set in Rome? 'So-crates', lecturing the old men on the Acropolis, is a case in point; he can't help looking like a Senator holding forth in the *curia*. Everyone's *heard* of his Athens, but not many people know or care what it *looks* like, and cinema has sensibly avoided running up big bills putting it on display.

Without an Athens as its iconic centre – an Athens that audiences would in any case read as a cheap Rome clone – film-makers are left wondering what, if anything, 'Greece' is supposed to look like; and unsure why, in any case, an audience would care to see it. Their solutions to these two fundamental obstacles are necessarily (and productively) varied, but almost invariably they are compelled to fall back on familiar tropes from Roman movies. The films that result from this accommodation to Rome – from imitating the 'imitation' – sometimes succeed in crafting an accessible storyline; but they can do so only by sidelining or even inverting the 'original' Greek narratives. Attempts to work around Rome produce fascinating failures. The remaining part of this chapter will consider three well-informed and distinctive films that tried to turn authentic Greece into good cinema. The films' breadth of range is usefully representative, and they have plenty going for them. They were made at the right time, the 1950s to 60s – the golden age of lavish ancient-world epic, from *Quo Vadis* (1951) to *Cleopatra* (1963). With one exception, money was not a problem. Their directors and scriptwriters were consummate professionals. Yet two of the three pictures are today despised by film buffs; and the third, for all its high production values, is mediocre as cinema. In all three cases, we'll see that Greece fails cinematically by not being like Rome; or by being too much like it; or, more often, both at once. Small wonder that each of the three directors vowed never to work with men in skirts again.

Atlas (1960)

Atlas starts with obvious and immediate advantages. Most obviously, it cashes in on the success of Greece's only really successful cinematic brand. At the time of the film's release, Steve Reeves' Hercules was raking it in at the US box office, kick-starting a bewilderingly productive craze for ancient musclemen. (This one would run and run; and we shall see in ch.2 that its consequences are still with us.) *Atlas* offers a Hercules clone with an equally impressive physique and a similar line in overthrowing tyrants. Atlas himself is a moderately famous mythical character in his own right, with a crucial cameo role in Hercules' own story; the film adds the spin that he is a better fighter than Hercules himself, having beaten him at the Olympics. (Classics buffs will recognize the aptness of the allusion: Hercules was the games' legendary founder.)

'Feared by Every Man – Desired by Every Woman!' The prospects are good for a crowd-pleasing yarn of rippling muscles and thrilling deeds, all presented in living colour (the poster is particularly garish: see Fig. 2) and widescreen VistaScope. There is the promise, too, of added value that will set the picture apart from the typical

2. 'Feared by Every Man – Desired by Every Woman!' (*Atlas*). But layered prior receptions rest heavily on the shoulders of the Greek action hero, predisposing audiences to mistrust him as straight male lead. Like *300*, *Atlas* is raining men.

sword-and-sandal saga. This revisionist version of Atlas isn't just a strongman; he's a restless soul, wandering the earth looking for answers to the human condition. This could turn out to be the thinking person's Hercules.

Additionally, *Atlas* has the distinction of having been directed and produced by the famous Roger Corman. A prototype of the recent crop of 'guerrilla' film-makers, this versatile and prolific hack director-*cum*-producer only lost money on one movie in his life, and *Atlas* was not it. Corman remains a popular figure within the industry; he may be caught in cameo roles in *Silence of the Lambs* (1991), *Philadelphia* (1993), *Apollo 13* (1995) and *Scream 3* (2000). Francis Ford Coppola, Martin Scorsese and James Cameron got their first breaks in the picture business under his tutelage. One keen student of Corman was the young George Lucas: years later, producer Gary Kurtz bragged to reporters that the thrill-heavy production aesthetic of *Star Wars* (1977) was really just a big-budget version of the Corman style.

Corman is a past master at identifying and exploiting the trend of the moment. Hell's Angels, women's prisons, space opera ... the list goes on and on, and he is always up to date. To promote *Atlas*, he placed full-page colour adverts in the trade press, inviting cinema proprietors to cash in on the muscleman craze: 'Let Atlas Lift your Boxoffice (*sic*) to New Heights'. Corman is also a favourite with fans, with many cult classics to his credit. In the same year as *Atlas*, Corman also brought out the original B-movie *Little Shop of Horrors* and the first of his stylish Poe adaptations, *House of Usher*. Artistically he was on a high. His hard-hitting and dramatically effective meditation on Southern racism, *The Intruder* (1961), is still highly regarded by critics. (It also, uniquely, failed to cover its costs.)

In 1960, the year of *Atlas*, Corman had at least six movies out – a good year by his standards, though not a record (1957 had been busier). In total, Corman has been involved in well over 300 movies to date. He retired from directing in the 1970s but seems busier than ever, mostly in the role of executive producer, where he continues to display a good eye for commercial possibilities. In the wake of *Gladiator*, he has turned to Ancient Rome, with the Russian straight-to-video *Gladiator* rip-off *The Arena* (2001), also called *Gladiatrix* (tagline: 'in an age of gladiators ... destiny lives at the end of a sword'), and generic sword-and-sandal fare with *The Barbarian* (2003). *Atlas* was in the safest possible pair of hands. It may have had a modest budget, but the frugal Corman was well used to that; he makes sure that all of it appears on-screen, gamely walking on as an anonymous spear-carrier to pad out the battle scenes.

Other talents credited in *Atlas* similarly promise well. The screenplay is by the witty and well-read Charles Griffith, who penned the original *Little Shop of Horrors* for Corman in the same year and later scripted Corman's biker epic *The Wild Angels* (1966) and the notorious *Death Race 2000* (1975) – both enduring cult classics. Griffith's involvement in *Atlas* extends to co-production. The cast, although largely consisting of Corman regulars and hired-in nonentities, is led by Michael Forrest as Atlas: he subsequently played the Greek god Apollo in the classic *Star Trek* episode 'Who Mourns for Adonais?' (This isn't the last time that *Star Trek* will enter our narrative.) Thirty-three years after saving Greece from the tyrant Praximedes, Forrest was still looking good enough to have sex with Madonna in the opening scene of *Body of Evidence* (1993), although his screen persona by now lacked the stamina to survive the ordeal; he is still getting steady work in voice-overs.

Atlas' most striking distinction (and apparent advantage) is its bid for authenticity via genuine Greek locations. Corman shot the film in Greece, working around actual ancient ruins, and with a largely local crew of Greeks and Italians. Several of the cast were Greek, including a 'premiere ballerina' of the Greek National Opera. Corman's decision to shoot against real backdrops is

probably motivated mainly by his trademark frugality and oppor-
tunism as a producer. (In the same year as *Atlas* he threw together
a dirt-cheap war film, *Ski Troop Attack*, out of footage from a school
skiing holiday.) All the same, as a director, Corman is alive to the
possibilities of the locations as a unique selling point; and scriptwriter Griffith makes the most of them throughout the film, right
from the opening credits:

> The producers wish to thank the government of Greece for their
> cooperation during the filming of this picture and especially for
> the permission to photograph the authentic locations.

Already, though, the film is helplessly undermining its own credentials as an authentic narrative of Greece. The credits play out
against a background of orange-tinted neoclassical statuary – not
even plausibly Roman, let alone Greek – and begin by panning
down from a muscularly upraised fist. This visual motif explicitly
recalls the credit sequence of Kubrick's Roman-themed *Spartacus*,
released earlier the same year. Further glaring Greco-Roman confu-
sions are swift to follow. Corman cuts from his credit advertising
'the authentic locations' to open the film with an establishing long
shot of a model and matte – the 'authentic' Greek city of Thinis,
complete with *Roman* amphitheatre and aqueduct.

For connoisseurs of anachronism, and of plain bad movies,
delights await. The Roman architectural trimmings are never far
away. At a victory banquet, complete with a Roman-style dancing
girl, Praximedes' female companion Candia attempts to convert
Atlas to the tyrant's cause with talk of the Roman-style 'granaries
and aqueducts' he will build with the spoils of war. Praximedes
manoeuvres the aged *archon* of beleaguered Thinis into an agreement to settle the war between their city-states by single combat.
Atlas, Praximedes' champion, is recruited at the Olympic games and
meets Thinis' champion in a Greek-style wrestling match; but the

setting is the amphitheatre – and its spectators sit in aisles labelled with angular Roman letters. Other, more ostentatiously 'Greek' motifs are handled awkwardly. In Praximedes we get a token Greek-style tyrant, who spends far too much of his time pontificating in Griffith's idea of sophistic rhetoric; and we are treated to, not one, but two Greek philosophers. Their dialogue is even worse. Even the most gung-ho of bit-part players can do little with it:

> For many as are the ills that are incident [sic] to the state you have not the gods to blame but you, yourselves; whenever you deliberate on the business of the state you distrust and dislike men of superior intelligence and cultivate instead the most depraved of the orators who come before you. For those of you who are concerned about this growing decadence in our democracy, there will be a dialogue at my home tomorrow.

A catty aside from Praximedes in the following scene reveals this soapbox philosopher to have been Socrates (presumably filling in time waiting for Bill and Ted).

More generally, and more seriously, the use of Greek locations turns out to be a liability rather than an asset. Uniquely in the annals of the *pepla*, Corman has actually taken his production to Hellas – and he still cannot make *Atlas* look like anyone's idea of ancient Greece. Part of the problem is financial. Corman's backer, a Greek tycoon, is alleged to have pulled out at the last minute, forcing the director to improvise; lack of money is evident at a number of points in the film. For scenes which require intact façades, such as the Socrates episode, Corman is forced to fall back on holiday villas. One villa in particular, with distinctive railings, is recycled as at least two nominally separate locations. (My guess would be that Corman and party were staying there.) Yet the slashed budget cannot be the whole story behind Corman's failure to generate a distinctive visual image of Greece. The villa is not the only recurring backdrop;

Corman also re-uses a range of bushes so often that the audience comes to recognise them as old friends. Villas cost, but bushes, surely, are free and plentiful. This failure of visual imagination is surprising, even paradoxical, given the strong sense of style and spectacle on display in other Corman pictures. (A notable example is *House of Usher*, which came out in the same year as *Atlas*.)

Corman's visual gaffes are fun, but it's unfair to single him out for blame or mockery – or to shift the blame to Griffith, his scriptwriter and co-producer. Contamination by themes and motifs from Roman movies will be a persistent problem, not only for *Atlas* but for the whole stunted genre of Greek films. *Atlas* quickly descends into unintended bathos, much to the delight of connoisseurs of kitsch, but its faults are symptomatic of difficulties faced by other films in the field. Corman is unable to make *Atlas* look Greek, not because he's filming on the cheap (although that doesn't help), but because popular culture has no clear visual idea of 'Greece' that he can appeal to – no idiom that he can invoke.

The only visual shorthands available to Corman are Roman – amphitheatres, aqueducts, funny numbers – and these constantly threaten to hijack his narrative. In a sense, it's almost inevitable that his visual language is reduced to shots of rocks and bushes. Thematic shorthands for Greece are readily available but, as Corman discovers, they tend to be cinematically unhelpful. What can you make philosophers *do* on screen? How can you make them *look* good doing it? Even tyrants get bogged down in showy speeches far too much of the time:

But remember, there's no firm line between creation and destruction. One cannot survive without the other.

Look at those columns. What strength it must take to stand against the wind and the rain, and the thunder of Zeus. Atlas, be glad that you're not a tyrant. You have nothing to do but wander the earth and search for the truth. Do you think you'll find it?

And criticisms of Corman as an opportunistic hack are beside the point: these are Corman's strengths. Corman is the *exemplary* hack, the anti-**auteur**, the king of cash-ins: his career is a near-endless list of unpretentious, inventive, workmanlike genre pictures that made their money back. Some of them are even artistic successes. If anyone could make a successful *peplum*, it would be Corman; and it's notable that, after *Atlas*, he never comes back for another shot at the genre. Even for the arch-opportunist, Greece is unfertile soil.

Corman can make almost anything into a watchable movie (even *Ski Troop Attack*); indeed, he's since done it for Rome (*The Arena*) in his usual efficient style. Why not Greece? *Atlas* suggests some provisional ideas which might well apply to other *pepla*. I suggest three initial areas of thought:

First, *look and feel*. Unlike 'Rome', cinema audiences lack a distinct *visual* idea of Greece to which a director can appeal. Corman, the master of opportunistic mise-en-scène, finds himself actually in Greece and *still* can't improvise a workable cinematic 'look' for Greece. Instead, Roman visual motifs creep in; and sometimes this has to be a good thing. Why torture a mainstream audience with a Greek alphabet and numerals when Roman equivalents can help them find their seating aisle in the arena so much more easily? This isn't just pedantry (although it's that too): fail to articulate a visually coherent mise-en-scène and you fail to persuade an audience to invest belief in your story.

Cinema audiences may have a limited set of *thematic* ideas about Greek history – tyrants, philosophers – but these don't work well visually. What's more, audiences are predisposed to find them boring: all talk, no action. The historical motifs commonly associated with Roman history – revolting slaves, revolting emperors – are a much safer bet. Perhaps more contamination here would have actually *helped* Corman's picture ...

Second, *plot and motivation*. Greek myth looks promising as a source of plot ideas; but it turns out to be surprisingly limited. Many of its heroes transfer very badly to the screen. Corman's *Atlas* runs up against this difficulty: Atlas is famous for standing still and holding up the earth – not helpful when movie stars are supposed to move. (We encounter a similar problem with a historical twist in *The Colossus of Rhodes*.) Griffith is reduced to turning Atlas into an ersatz Hercules within an improvised plot. Overall, the most promising source of photogenic action-adventure narrative is the myth-peddling epic poet Homer, one of the very few Greek authors to maintain significant 'brand recognition' in Western mass culture. (Tellingly, Matt Groening's *The Simpsons* name-drops the bard in an *Odyssey*-themed episode.) But even Homer proves surprisingly intractable as Hollywood material, as Wolfgang Petersen recently found out in *Troy*. (More on this shortly, with *Helen of Troy* (1956).)

Questions of source material aside, *Atlas'* problems of plot and motivation are subordinate to a larger problem, which affects other film-makers as badly as it does Corman; digging around for a less awkward myth would hardly have helped him. What are Greeks to *do* in a film, except talk the plot to death? In the popular imagination, Romans win and lose empires, fight fur-clad barbarians and bring on the dancing girls. Greeks discuss the nature of the Good or flirt with underage boys. For very different reasons, neither of these activities makes good mainstream cinema.

Third, *discourse*: 'the film itself' is one thing, what people say about it quite another. *Atlas* actually isn't as bad as all that: it is competently shot, given the very tight budget. Nor is it as badly written as critics tend to assert. As the film stands, there is too much ponderous dialogue, but Griffith's script is literate and often thoughtful. It is also surprisingly well-informed on some aspects of classical antiquity. Griffith's 'Thinis' must derive its name from the Hellenistic Greek Thinite district of Egypt; the reference is incorrect but it's impressively obscure. At times the erudition is handled with a light touch. Praximedes' kiss is judged by Candia, priestess of Hygieia, as 'like the kiss of Apollo – carved by Pheidias'. Some at least of the ridicule that continues to be heaped upon *Atlas* is not justified by the picture itself.

This ongoing caricature of *Atlas* by critics / fans (the distinction is increasingly meaningless in the internet age) is in part a symptom of popular culture's prejudices and anxieties about Greekness. This is not the last occasion on which we shall see a picture written off suspiciously quickly. Rarely well funded and often just a little shambolic, *pepla* make very convenient scapegoats within a much wider *discourse* – Western culture's larger ongoing conversation with itself about (who gets to decide) what Ancient Greece means (and for whom). Films like *Atlas* are important for reception studies because they ask us to decide what we are in it for – film criticism, or (my answer) cultural studies?

Or perhaps a little bit of both, if only to give Corman's picture a sympathetic hearing for once in its life. An ambitious film made in the teeth of horrifying difficulties, *Atlas* is an easy target for critical scorn. Instead, Corman deserves qualified praise: he persevered, improvised, and finished the picture when a lesser director (or a self-important 'auteur') would have given up. Some of its problems could have been resolved had the money come through as promised; it is tantalising to speculate on what might have been (better voice synchronisation, decent action sequences, some editing to keep the dialogue in proportion). And the film's disastrous aspects are easily over-stated. Despite its deficiencies, it did break even – not difficult, given how little money went into it. There was even an Italian imitator, *Atlas in the Land of the Cyclops* (1961). A couple of cheap

Italian strongman pictures were also re-branded as 'Atlas' films for the US market, cashing in on *Atlas*' modest success: local action hero Maciste becomes *Atlas Against the Czar* (1963), and his rival Ursus is *Son of Atlas in the Valley of the Lions* (1961). (Ursus and Maciste will return in our next chapter, 'Mythconceptions'.)

Nevertheless, the movie's poor reception did its participants no favours. Sascha Dario, 'premiere ballerina', seems never to have appeared on screen again. Frank Wolff, a saturnine and superbly cynical Praximedes, only made films in Italy after *Atlas*. (Was he head-hunted by one of Corman's Italian crew?) He committed suicide in Rome in 1971.

The Colossus of Rhodes (1961)

My second example sounds, at first, as though it ought to be a terrible mistake. A sword-and-sandal picture directed and co-written by famous spaghetti-western auteur *Sergio Leone*? No wonder film buffs have been quick to write it off as an early aberration; and it is true that the film has plenty of problems.

Again, though, *The Colossus of Rhodes* is not nearly as bad as has been made out, and its director is actually very well qualified to throw together a successful *peplum*. Leone has achieved lasting fame for stylish, atmospheric late-sixties westerns including *A Fistful of Dollars*, *The Good, the Bad and the Ugly* and *Once Upon a Time in the West*; but he came late to the western. Cinema was a family trade in which he had been working since the early forties, starting as a child actor but picking up assistant-director credits by his late teens. One of his early stints as assistant director was the acclaimed *Fabiola* (1949), a cinematically ambitious remake of a 1916 silent classic (itself based on a pious Victorian novel) of Christians facing martyrdom in the arena. Leone went on to carve out a now little-known directorial career in high-concept sword-

and-sandal, working (usually uncredited) on most of the famous Roman blockbusters of the 1950s-60s golden age. He was second-unit director on *Quo Vadis* (1951), on *Helen of Troy* (1956), and even on William Wyler's Oscar-hogging *Ben-Hur* (1959). Leone moved up to assistant director for *Aphrodite, Goddess of Love* (1958) and *The Last Days of Pompeii* (1959). He had also learned how to write for the period, contributing to the screenplays of *Aphrodite* and *Last Days*, along with the earlier *Sign of the Gladiator* (1958). Corman had come to the *peplum* as the ultimate B-movie improviser; Leone was perhaps the most experienced specialist of his day in scripting and directing the ancient world.

The film he comes up with when he turns to ancient Greece has many strong points; it is undeniably a much better picture than *Atlas*. The premise is commercially astute, thanks to the bankable fame of one of the greatest lost landmarks of antiquity. The title also pitches the film at the established market for spaghetti epics. 'Colossus' is a stock name for sub-Herculean strongmen, as seen in the previous year's *Colossus and the Amazon Queen* and *Colossus and the Huns*. The direction, needless to say, is energetic and stylish. Leone makes striking and effective use of camera movement (pans and tracking shots), and of low angles at key moments. He is a confident and experienced visual story-teller, able to guide us through an engagingly complex plot, balancing moments of tension against lighter scenes. The film's often dark ambience is greatly enhanced by Angelo Lavagnino's atmospheric score; by turns exciting and haunting, it sympathetically matches Leone's pacing throughout the picture. The dialogue is merely adequate and the performances two-dimensional; but the cast and the many extras attack the physical aspects of their roles with enthusiasm and enable some exciting set-pieces. Locations are used intelligently, giving a strong sense of epic scale; and they are complemented by striking and cost-effective set design. Coupling these sets and models with his trademark inventive camera angles, Leone is able to conjure up an imposing and credible Colossus. Finally, the film's visual effects are imaginative and convincingly implemented; they contribute to some memorably macabre moments. Highlights include a genuinely disturbing torture scene; an exciting last-minute rescue by rebel archers; and a tense attempted escape by ship, in which burning pitch is dropped from the Colossus to engulf the heroes in clinging fire. The best scene is daringly original: the hero Dario duels with the villain's bodyguards on the shoulder and arm of the Colossus itself, before making a high dive into the harbour mouth below.

On the debit side, the romantic-triangle subplot is a non-starter. Torn (allegedly) between the alluring Diala and the politically committed Mirte, the virile Athenian warrior Dario can only fix a rictus-like smirk on his face, guffaw heartily, and pretend he's having an interesting time. Dario is playing at being a muscularly pagan Roman conqueror, but the relationship really needs a virtuous Christian girl to make the sparks fly.

Dario: Are you looking for someone?
Mirte: I see I wasn't too subtle.

Pagan girls are just too easy: Diala fobs Dario off at first, but only because it amuses her to play games with the hunky visitor. Without a feisty Christian girl to resist them, men in skirts come across as just, well, gay – in either, or indeed both, of the word's current popular meanings (homosexual / tragically square). Hollywood's narratives of pagan boys and Christian girls in wicked Rome manage to deliver an erotic charge by throwing together two mutually attracted but spiritually incompatible young people. His and her inability to see eye to eye not only makes the relationship more interestingly edgy, it also provides a ready-made excuse for the deferral of a sexual relationship. This rationale made Hollywood's toga epics an ideal match to the market conditions of the time.

The films top and tail the reign of the Hays Code, a nasty piece of industry self-censorship that ran from the mid-thirties to sixties: its first principle was that 'no picture shall be produced that will lower the moral standards of those who see it'. 'Low forms of sex relationship' were to be castigated, and 'sex perversion' swept under the carpet; religion and 'correct standards of life' were to be treated with reverence. With their essentially Victorian storylines, the toga films became perfect Code-era properties with only a little fine-tuning – the only alteration needed was to tone down the dancing girls and asses'-milk baths of the genre's earlier decades. Imperial Rome wooed the lucrative family market via sports, action and romance, set Christian virtue centre-stage, and put pagan vice firmly in its place. Consequently, a routine Roman epic such as *Quo Vadis* (1951) makes obvious romantic / sexual sense, at least to its contemporary audience. The hero and heroine aren't sleeping together yet because her mind is on higher things; she's saving herself for later. This deferral helps get the plot under way; frustration leads easily to conflict, and thus to exciting stuff happening. But the form it takes also reassures the audience that, despite appearances, the man in the pleated miniskirt is probably not gay after all.

Hollywood's Greece, set hundreds of years before any Christian girls are available for the sexual frustration of young male pagans, immediately faces problems. If *he* is pagan and likes girls, and if *she* is pagan and likes boys, why don't they spend the whole movie in bed? Porn directors rely on just this assumption when they set films in a Christianity-free Rome: everyone is 'pagan', therefore sex-obsessed. (The Romans, who were both pagan and very proper, would have been shocked at this suggestion.) So, why no straight Greek porn? One major reason has to be that Rome has already cornered the market in ancient heterosexual romance via Victorian historical melodrama – a topic to which we'll shortly return; but, as we'll see, that is not the whole story.

Visually, Leone faces some problems. An excellent director of action, he gets the best from his crowds of extras, juggling locations and sets with conviction; but he is badly let down by his set dressers and costumiers. The cast wear a motley assortment of home-spun cloaks, off-the-shoulder mini-tunics and cuirasses loaded with ridiculous brooches and bosses, the apparent cast-offs of Roman-themed kitsch like *Demetrius and the Gladiators* (1954). Typically, the men are showing really far too much leg (especially given the legs in question). Rhodes' soldiers wear the bright red cloaks of cinema's Roman legionaries, and some are equipped with Roman-style segmented body armour. King Serse can only keep up appearances as a wicked king by taking hair and wardrobe tips from various screen Neros. And the palace décor puts these sartorial difficulties in the shade. We can spot an ill-assorted jumble of classical and Hellenistic Greek knick-knacks at various points in the picture: statues, pots, a bust of Alexander, and – bizarrely – a slab of the Parthenon frieze. But much of the visual clutter in the background of scenes isn't Greek at all. We see millennia-old Minoan tourist tat, including an oversized copy of the famous 'snake goddess' statuette; the bodies of King Serse's ancestors in the royal mausoleum, mummified Egyptian-style; what looks very much like a bust of Augustus, first emperor of Rome (nearly three centuries ahead of schedule); and a striking pair of faux-Assyrian winged bulls. The winged bulls are part of the exotic décor of the Rhodian temple of Baal, no less, which also features a lion-mouth portal and standard-issue flaming pit straight out of the pulp serials.

The film reaches its climax in a Roman-style amphitheatre (yet another ersatz Colosseum) unconvincingly Greeked-up by sticking plaster lions adapted from Mycenae's Lion Gate behind the imperial – or, in this case, royal – box. Pointy-bearded henchmen harass the rebel prisoners (it's a long story) from Roman-style chariots, complete with the axle-mounted scythe blades we last saw in

Ben-Hur (1959). The chariots, too, are given a superficial Greek identity by pasting a decorative border onto the bodywork. Visually, the scene is a mess.

There are further difficulties. The film's narrative is bewilderingly complex: the plot builds towards a multiple surprise ending, with twist following on twist, and an over-large ensemble of named characters makes it hard to follow what's going on. This near-frantic urge to keep the screen busy is forced upon the scriptwriters by their certified A-list star – not Rory Calhoun, a B-list Hollywood leading man, best known for his role in *How to Marry a Million-aire* (1953), but the Colossus itself. As a paid-up Wonder of the Ancient World, the Colossus – like Atlas, the legendary strongman – ought to have cinematic potential. (After all, the original statue was a blockbusting attraction in classical antiquity.) Like Atlas, though, the Colossus is famous for standing still (and, after a while, falling down) rather than for *doing* anything. The film-makers are commendably inventive in getting around this, transforming the statue into a two-legged fortress that bestrides the harbour mouth to defend Rhodes from invasion – and tweaking history to make the Colossus topple at a dramatically appropriate moment. But, like *Atlas*, the resulting movie feels too improvised. It raids the sword-and-sandal toy-box indiscriminately, pulling out story-telling devices as ill-assorted as its set dressing. One of the film's less awkward thefts is the character of Carete, the inventor of the secret weapons built into the Colossus; he is an off-the-shelf Archimedes who is more or less at home in the film's Hellenistic setting. But without Romans to defend the city against (as Archimedes did at Syracuse) his inventions have to find Greek enemies – and, in doing so, inspire additional gratuitous plot twists. Other incidental borrowings from Rome include a scene in which the wicked king and his cronies plan to use the Colossus to shield Phoenician pirates. The piracy theme is another *Ben-Hur* leftover; and the mise-en-scène, as the tyrant

Leaders of Rhodes look at a scale model of the Colossus, spectacula

ress-statue that will guard the Harbor of Rhodes.

RHODES " In SupertotalScope
and EASTMANCOLOR

roperty of National Screen Service Corp. Licensed for display only in connection with
ne exhibition of this picture at your theatre. Must be returned immediately thereafter. 61/170

3. Mixed-up tyrant 'Serse' (*The Colossus of Rhodes*) makes like Nero. The background clutter may be ostensibly Greek, but the audience reads the *mise-en-scène* – and the storyline – squarely in terms of best-selling Roman narratives, particularly *Quo Vadis'* Rome/Neropolis.

Crowds gather at the port of Rhodes to see the arrival of

4. 'Crowds gather at the port' (*The Colossus of Rhodes*) – edging the notional star out of the frame. You can just see the Colossus' feet at top left. Roman mise-en-scène (legionary-style red cloaks, segmented armour) invades the screen. We'll see those cloaks again in *300*.

e ship, brought in under heavy guard.

RHODES " In SupertotalScope and EASTMANCOLOR

and his confidants gather round a model of the harbour area, is lifted wholesale from the thematically similar 'Neropolis' scene in the Roman blockbuster *Quo Vadis* (1951) (Fig. 3).

The iffy costuming and props are a variant on the same general problem that we saw Corman run into with his choice of locations, a problem that no production team can escape: what is Greece supposed to *look* like? Roman visual motifs often push the notional Greek subject to the edge of the frame – sometimes quite literally (Fig. 4). And the near-frantic urge to keep the screen busy with incident reflects a similar overlap. What are Greeks supposed to *do*? Stand very still? That's not cinema; we want movies that move. Leone's *Colossus* raises additional questions which are equally broadly applicable. Philosophy and boys aside, what are Greeks supposed to *talk* about, if they're not to sound 'all Greek' to the audience? Indeed, who *are* these 'Greeks'? Where *is* 'Greece', exactly?

Wherever it is, it's not Rhodes; the script establishes the Rhodians as separate from a Greece championed by the Athenian, Dario. (Leone and his colleagues implicitly concede Thucydides' point about Greece's too-fiddly geography and politics.) Even Dario seems an unlikely Hellene; his name is an Italianised form of Darius, the famous Persian aggressor against Greece, aligning him with the wicked king Serse (an Italianised form of Darius' son Xerxes, as in Handel's opera *Serse*). We can guess at the notional Greek names of some characters. Rebel leader 'Lissipu', who dreams of overthrowing the Colossus, must be Lysippus – an unintentionally ironic choice, given that he shares his name with a sculptor famous for (among other things) making colossal statues. Many of the rest (e.g. pointy-bearded young villain 'Thara') just sound made-up.

The Colossus is hardly very Greek either, and for a more surprising reason. The image of the titanic statue bestriding the harbour mouth turns out not to be ancient after all; no ancient author alleged anything of the sort. Instead, the image first emerges in Renaissance woodcuts, and has been reproduced more or less trustingly ever since. (The site's archaeology, of course, supplies no distinct visual image; the Colossus fell in an earthquake in antiquity, just as Leone alleges.) It would be unfair to criticise Leone for failing to have checked this; *The Colossus of Rhodes* is just a movie, and most viewers will be perfectly happy with his bandy-legged bronze giant. Nonetheless, it is undeniable that Leone's Colossus is already a Renaissance reception, seen through a glass darkly, long before his Carete first puts stylus to wax tablet. The film thinks it's referring back to Greek history; actually it gets no further than the imagination of a sixteenth-century book illustrator.

Colossus was by no means a disaster, commercially or even artistically; it is visually imaginative, and delivers striking set-pieces. All the same, it seems clear that the experience helped persuade Leone to back away from sword-and-sandal work – and particularly from *pepla*. His only subsequent screenwriting co-credit on a subject from the ancient world was the Romulus-and-Remus biopic *Duel of the Titans*, made more or less at the same time as *Colossus* (1961). He also signed on as second-unit director on Robert Aldrich's unintentionally hilarious *Last Days of Sodom and Gomorrah* (1962). ('Beware Sodomite patrols!') Leone never made another film set in ancient Greece.

Helen of Troy (1956)

My third and final example is a very different proposition. Although rarely seen these days, *Helen of Troy* is tolerably well regarded by critics. While it shows its age, verdicts on the film still tend to be charitable – quite unlike the scorn routinely heaped on *Atlas* and *The Colossus of Rhodes*. *Helen*'s director, the formidable and versatile Robert Wise, came out of the experience comparatively unscathed, although he publicly swore off the ancient world in perpetuity, and continued to build a distinguished Hollywood career. Wise had cut his teeth as editor for Orson Welles on his Oscar-winners *Citizen Kane* (1941) and *The Magnificent Ambersons* (1942), and had been in the director's chair since 1944; he continued making films into the late 1980s. Highlights of his career include *The Body Snatcher* (1945) and science-fiction classic *The Day the Earth Stood Still* (1951); also, surprisingly, the musicals *West Side Story* (1959) and *The Sound of Music* (1965), both Oscar-winners.

Helen even became the subject of two 'remakes' of sorts, in Wolfgang Petersen's *Troy* and a straight-to-DVD *Helen of Troy* that made it to market in time to capitalise on the Petersen media circus. (As such, it lays useful groundwork for consideration of other 'remakes' in chs 2 and 3 below.) The picture stands head and shoulders above *Atlas* and *Colossus* as a full-blown Hollywood epic, with lavish production values and a budget to match. However, it does supply *Atlas* with one important cue. The gimmick of Corman's picture was to be its return to the material record (ruined temples). Wise's *Helen* revisited the textual record, in the form of Homer's definitive epic poem, the *Iliad*. The film bills itself explicitly as an adaptation of Homer – a claim that Petersen was to recycle for his twenty-first century epic.

We'll see various sword-and-sandal efforts billing themselves as 'adaptations' of Greek classics in ch.2 below, though none of them carry it off with anything like *Helen*'s conviction and integrity. The script is by classicist Hugh Gray; he was later to do excellent work (again creatively reworking Homer) on the Kirk Douglas *Ulysses* (1955), still a cult classic. Gray's presence in the opening credits underwrites the film's claims to authenticity right from the start; he turns in a script which demonstrates its respect for the textual sources by engaging with them knowledgeably and creatively. In parts, the film is not so much an adaptation of the *Iliad* as a nuanced and well-informed – and quite 'classical' – response to its challenges.

Although some scenes from the epic are transferred to the screen quite faithfully, the film as a whole is almost an anti-*Iliad*.

The Trojans are the heroes. The effete troublemaker Paris is transformed into a romantic hero in the classic Hollywood idiom, hopelessly devoted to a virtuous Helen. Gray's guiltless heroine is herself an echo of ancient revisionist treatments (e.g. Euripides' half-comical tragedy, *Helen*) which sought to shift the blame for the war off her shoulders. And the Greeks come off badly, just as they did in some later Greek versions of the Troy story. The script emphasises the dark aspects of the warrior chieftain Achilles, the hero of Homer's epic, playing down Homer's sympathetic insights into his disillusionment and grief. In the film, he becomes a sadistic and seemingly unstoppable villain – a Bronze-Age Terminator, manipulated into vendetta by the clever and amoral Greek leaders Agamemnon and Menelaus. Gray has been criticised for his un-Homeric characterisations of the brothers, but that is to miss the point: his revisionist characterisations demonstrate a deep knowledge of the ancient sources that goes beyond the obvious. His cynical, manipulative Agamemnon and Menelaus are strikingly faithful to Euripides' characterisation of the brothers in his tragedy, *Iphigenia at Aulis*. The casting as Achilles of British actor Stanley Baker – already familiar to cinema audiences from a series of villainous hard-man roles – underlines the script's shift of sympathy. (Baker's career didn't suffer from his appearance here. He even revisited Greek mythic history, albeit at the opposite end of the story, as the Macedonian general Attalus in Robert Rossen's well-regarded 1956 *Alexander the Great*.)

Helen of Troy particularly shines as a thoughtful, literate screenplay, with Gray showing his trademark cleverness in mixing and matching non-obvious sources. His Paris, for instance, is written as the polar opposite of Euripides' Hippolytus: the pathological misogynist of Euripides' play refuses to worship Aphrodite, while Gray's romantic hero worships her almost exclusively. There are treats for classicists in the revisionist characterisations at Priam's court; pious Aeneas is a womaniser and diplomatic liability in this version of the story, while Paris' dutiful elder brother Hector is now a simple-minded sports fanatic. Paris comes off very well by comparison; in particular, he picks up Hector's good points as a statesman and patriot. His arrival on Sparta's shores via shipwreck is a typical Gray moment: Homer is the source, but not the *Iliad*. Instead Paris steals a scene from Odysseus as he first appears in the *Odyssey*, found storm-tossed on a beach by the bold princess Nausicaa – or, in this case, by a similarly feisty Helen.

The film's merits don't end there. It is well played, with satisfying performances from the usual suspects, including white-bearded toga veteran Harry Andrews as Laocoon. The production design puts plenty of money on screen, and goes some way towards solving the problem of what Greece looks like. If anything the challenge is more acute here. This is the mythic Greece of prehistory, not the Classical Greece of hoplites and flute-girls familiar from Attic pots; and the designers must simultaneously create a distinctive and plausible look for the Greeks' Eastern enemies, the Trojans. The success is only partial; none of the costumes look at all 'authentic', even to a non-specialist audience. Wise's recreation of Troy, on the other hand, is an imaginative and thematically resonant success story. Again, Hugh Gray's scholarly touch is subtly evident here. Taking his cue from the nineteenth- and early twentieth-century excavations by Heinrich Schliemann and Arthur Evans, and the mountain of scholarship that followed in their wake, he implicitly chooses to identify Homer's Greek 'Achaeans' with the historical Mycenaeans – and gives his Trojans a built environment which closely resembles that of the historical Minoans, a wealthy trading culture which, just like Troy, lost out to the Mycenaean hegemony. With its squat red-ochre columns and idyllic frescos, the Troy of

Hugh Gray and Robert Wise is the spitting image of the famous 'Palace of Minos' recreated by Evans at Knossos.

This, then, is a highly professional production in every aspect. In some areas, it is more than competent: it is inspired. It is thoughtful and evocative in its responses to Homer, to ancient Greek literature as a whole, and even to a difficult area of modern scholarship. In many ways, it's clearly unfair to lump *Helen* in with *Atlas* and *The Colossus of Rhodes*. Yet, despite its undeniable successes in some areas, the film shares some of their basic failings. Its success in creating a visual image for Greece is patchy; in fact, the production design only really hits its stride when it turns its attention to Greece's enemy, Troy.

There is also one area at least in which *Helen* fails where *Atlas* and *Colossus* succeed: it is not much fun. Corman and Leone surmounted one of the perennial problems – what are Greeks to *do*? – by improvising plots that border at times on the ridiculous; but at least they succeed in motivating action, and plenty of it. *Helen of Troy*, fatally respectful towards its classical sources, drags. What is worse, the film ends up falling between two stools. On the one hand, as a well-intentioned adaptation of the *Iliad*, it is bound to seem slow; not enough happens for a movie audience's liking. In its accommodation to the time-tried Hollywood formula of a romantic hero and heroine, on the other hand, Wise's film is bound to ring false. Menelaus and Agamemnon are indeed nasty pieces of work and Achilles a figure of menace in some ancient versions; but Paris, a hero? More recently, *Troy* tries to fix this, but only succeeds in shifting the problem elsewhere (in ch.2 below, *Helen* is useful background to understanding what went wrong there).

The romantic premise is in any case doomed by another recurring problem. Outside of porn, pagan leading men can't fulfil their Hollywood ambitions as cruel and virile hunks if the script pairs them off with worldly-wise and 'easy' pagan women. To get the sparks flying and the plot rolling, what they really need is a feisty Christian girl with an urge to save their souls. Hollywood's formula for ancient-world romance is effectively the same as that used by Mills and Boon; there is no storyline without an initially starchy heroine and a handsome male lead who strikes her as mad, bad and dangerous to know. All the best stories in Greek history happen much too early to fit any Christians into the plot. If anything, *Helen of Troy* is an extreme example, set as it is well over a thousand years BC. Helen and Paris need some tension and misunderstanding in their relationship if it is to drive the plot (and if Paris isn't to be thought a sissy for wearing a skirt). Instead, as two pagans in a world where no-one is anything else, they are too bland and lovey-dovey even to interest us. Meanwhile, on a larger structural level, Troy's peace-loving citizens fill in unconvincingly as 'Christians' being persecuted by aggressive, imperialist 'Romans' (the Mycenaean invaders). Perversely, then, the film ends up as a kind of toga movie by default, lapsing into the familiar clichés while simultaneously rejecting the erotic friction that gives the Roman Hollywood blockbusters their spark. It keeps the bathwater but throws out the baby.

Gray's painstaking mise-en-scène cannot paper over these very obvious cracks. Despite his thoroughly excellent work, the film is neither persuasive (as a historical drama) nor satisfying (as a romantic epic). *Helen of Troy* is partially successful: it looks good, in a static way, and contains some strong performances. But as a cinematic experience it is badly flawed, fit fodder for Plato's Cave; and its flaws seem to arise inevitably from the collision between standard Hollywood narrative practice and the myths of ancient Greece.

Greece is not the word: Cleopatra in the Bible Belt

Even allowing for awkward and sometimes laughable accommoda-tions to Hollywood and to Rome, Greek movies are hard to sell to movie audiences. Building on our initial ideas, some of the stories we might now tell to explain this are:

Cities. Greece has no distinctive 'urban image'. For all its efforts in self-promotion, from classical antiquity onwards, Athens is not synonymous with Greece; and Athens itself is no Rome, no Babylon. Thucydides vastly over-rates its kerb appeal. Roman literary and popular cultures were self-consciously urban even in antiquity. Through satire and panegyric, inscriptions and graffiti, Rome wrote itself into history as the one and only *Urbs* – the metropolis, the Big City, the centre of events. Tellingly, both Babylon and Rome have explicitly been invoked as exemplars for and by Hollywood. In the heyday of the studio system, directors of ancient-world blockbusters explicitly compared themselves to Roman emperors, offering grand and gory spectacles to the *plebs* in the arena of cinema; Cecil B. De Mille is the most notorious auteur to play at Nero but he is by no means alone. (Amateur creators can now copy De Mille copying Nero, circulating their home videos via the CD-burning software 'Nero: Burning ROM'.) And Kenneth Anger's *Hollywood Babylon* remains the classic exposé of film-star kinks. Athens – too fragmentary, too small, too wound up in the history of cinema-unfriendly Ideas – fails to measure up. I have suggested that cinema's avoidance of Athens makes good commercial sense. The two cities' very different later histories aside (and philhellene nostalgia has always gone hand in glove with contempt for an Athens vitiated by Ottoman dominance), why throw large budgets at a set that audiences will always interpret as a second-rate knock-off of designer Rome? It is worth noting in passing that none of the films in this book is set in Athens. This urban absence leaves Greece without any distinctive 'look and feel' in the contemporary popular imagination. No wonder all *Atlas* can do, at short notice and on next to no budget, is stumble around in the shrubbery.

Sex. There are a thousand stories in the Naked City of Holly-wood's Rome – and most of them are about sex and violence, made palatable for the Bible belt with a veneer of non-denominational early Christian piety. Without the pull of the metropolis and with no Christians expected for centuries, Greece is hard to sell on sex – or, at any rate, on the right kind of sex (orgies, gladiators, dancing girls). Stereotypically 'Greek' vices (boys, Socratic dialogue) are impossible to package for a mainstream cinema-going public. The same public finds it hard to swallow the idea of a lustfully hetero-sexual ancient Greek; we've already seen some possible reasons for this. Meanwhile, Romans sell conventional sex by the shelf-load. There is an academic article to be written some day about the rash of post-*Gladiator* porn films – all recycling *Gladiator's* iconic Colos-seum as a sales hook for 'dickus maximus' (*sic*). Romans deliver the ultimate Hollywood combo: Sex *and* the City.

Sources. Hollywood's Rome has always been able to lift plots and characters from a vast store of more or less tacky Victorian recep-tions. Starting life as blockbuster novels, lavish stage productions ('toga plays') or even scripted firework spectaculars ('pyrodrama', an important source for the 1935 *The Last Days of Pompeii*), these exciting and colourful stories were naturals for film adaptation. Often the narratives have been re-used several times along the way. *Ben-Hur* was a best-selling novel, then a big-budget staged drama, then three separate film productions; similar stories lie behind films such as *Quo Vadis* and *Sign of the Cross*. The toga formula hooked Victorian readers and audiences by combining the wholesome moral lessons of evangelical Christianity with a licence to enjoy pagan Rome's soft-focus depravity, without fear of moral contamination. Knowing that history guaranteed Rome's decline and fall – and that, in the meantime, the Christians were guaranteed at least a moral victory – respectable Victorians could sit back and feast their eyes on Rome's doomed pleasures with a clear conscience. Hollywood was

quick to catch on to this ready-made excuse for showing the ascendancy of virtue over wickedness. In the process, they blew most of
the budget on the wickedness, just as the Victorians had done; in
terms of mise-en-scène, virtue comes much cheaper than dancing
girls and chariot races.

So-crates. Audiences are resistant to a Greece closely associated
with the history of ideas. Throw us an establishing shot of the
Acropolis, and we think Philosophy, Art, Democracy – and switch
off. *Bill and Ted*'s Athens episode knows exactly what our reaction is likely to be; paradoxically and very cleverly, it maintains
our interest by acting out our *loss* of interest via cinematography.
Modern popular culture's suspicion of intellectual elitism – which in
part, at least, has to be a healthy reaction to centuries of being told
what is good for us by a classically educated elite – has unfortunate
side-effects for receptions of ancient Greece. Hollywood's problem
is particularly acute when it comes to its home market, the USA,
where the university establishment has set up Socrates and Co.
as the unwitting linch-pins in a conservatively framed 'Western
Tradition'. This invented tradition is at once a bandwagon (for reac-
tionaries allergic to cultural diversity) and a bugbear (for liberals
and for anyone who has to sit the lecture courses). Additionally,
'Greek' has been appropriated as a tendentious shorthand for the
privileged education and artificially enhanced material prospects of
America's social elite. The Ivy League fraternity system flaunts its
faux-highbrow exclusivity via an ostentatious use of Greek letters in
its nomenclature. Phis, Deltas, Kappas and all the rest, potentially
ad nauseam; there's plenty here for a mass audience to resent. (It is
worth noting, too, that the actual *fun* these 'Greek' fraternities have
is emphatically coded Roman: the 'toga party' is the ultimate cliché
of frat-house excess.) Any attempt to breathe cinematic life into
ancient Greece has to take account of this excess and unwelcome
baggage.

The dead weight of these accidental but ultimate Dead White European Males has obvious consequences for Hollywood decision-making. Occasionally, Greek material is sneaked in briefly to raise the tone and then hustled quickly out of the picture. It can be very useful in papering over a thin plot; Greek mythology, in particular, is full of impressive-sounding names that can make a film seem momentarily less stupid. (Techno-thriller novels often use the same trick, for identical reasons; think of all those waiting-room staples with titles like *The Icarus Manifesto*.) We might think, for instance, of *Mission: Impossible 2*'s 'Chimera' virus and its antidote 'Bellerophon'. *M:I-2* more or less gets away with this; the film is already such a pretentious mess that a sprinkling of Classics Lite can't do much additional harm. But the gambit always carries with it the risk of a headlong collapse into bathos.

Even within notionally 'Greek' narratives, Greece's baggage of motifs and themes is typically traded in for something more audience-friendly. The Romanised visual images of *The Colossus of Rhodes* and *Atlas* are examples of a fairly typical response. Film-makers, despairing of selling Greece as a cinematic product, turn to Rome for window-dressing; and these imported visual cues in turn deform the 'original' story, cueing the audience to read the plot against toga-movie codes and values (a comparison from which it is bound to emerge as distinctly second-rate). At times, it seems that anything goes – as long as it's not Greek.

Twentieth-century versions of the *Cleopatra* story are a case in point. The historical Cleopatra VII was the last of the Ptolemies, a Macedonian dynasty, founded by one of Alexander's generals, that ruled Egypt for nearly three centuries: her cultural identity was pretty solidly 'Greek'. She played at Pharaoh for domestic consumption, even learning to speak Egyptian, which was more than any of her ancestors had done; but she had nothing in common with Egypt's majority population. Marc Antony's biographer, Plutarch, tells us that Cleopatra spoke seven languages in all; the diplomatically crucial one was of course Greek. As a cosmopolitan Mediterranean monarch, she looked outward toward a larger Hellenistic world, increasingly to the emerging superpower of Rome. So why do we think of her as an exotic and irresistible Egyptian?

A century of film and layered **star image** can claim much of the credit. J. Gordon Edwards' famous lost silent epic for Fox (1917) repackaged Cleopatra as a harem temptress by casting Hollywood's original superstar vamp, 'Theda Bara', an American shopgirl reinvented by Fox studio publicists in semi-pornographic style as the fatal daughter of an Eastern potentate (her screen name is an anagram of 'Arab Death'). But if Bara's star image orientalised Cleopatra's pop-culture persona, the surviving plot synopsis makes it clear that her story was largely Romanised – a kiss-and-tell history of the late Republic (Antony, Caesar, the First Triumvirate, Actium). Only Romans can muster the necessary eye-candy for epic spectacle. (A cast of thousands! Eighty real ships!) Cecil B. DeMille's 1934 *Cleopatra*, made for Paramount and starring Claudette Colbert, finds other ways of giving way to Rome. Cleopatra, previously a strong-minded career girl, meets her match in a virile Roman 'Mr Wrong' – but not before shopping till she drops in the exclusive boutiques of the metropolis (an echo of Theda Bara's fifty-plus costume changes). Like Athens, Greek Alexandria isn't big enough for a thirties city girl.

Edwards' silent classic suffered a remake of sorts in Fox's infamous 1963 *Cleopatra*, directed by Joseph K. Mankiewicz and starring Elizabeth Taylor and Richard Burton. Again, Egypt and Rome own the plot; Greece is invisible. Cleopatra's Alexandria is dominated by a moodily-lit palace stuffed with Middle Kingdom trimmings; Liz Taylor, bringing with her more real-life baggage than is good for her or the role, gives us a Cleo with a heavy kohl habit. Superficially, Technicolor and sound give the queen more of a say; but, just as in 1917 and 1934, the plot is all about Rome. (There are scattered and unresolved hints at a pan-Mediterranean political agenda for Cleopatra; perhaps the sub-plot ended up on the cutting-room floor, shed by a panicked Fox as they frantically tried to cut a viable film out of the bloated mess served up by Mankiewicz and producer Walter Wanger.) The director's original hope to divide the footage up into two films, *Caesar and Cleopatra* and *Antony and Cleopatra*, only rubs the message in. Cleopatra is glamour – and, in this, she's more Roman than the Romans – but Caesar and Antony drive the plot.

As the spoof *Carry on Cleo* put it a year after Mankiewicz's botched epic, 'Certain liberties have been taken with Cleopatra'. The last of the Ptolemies has seen her bloodline, her culture, even her mother tongue written out of the picture. Her Greek name means 'her father's glory' but she has been recast by Roman narratives into an oriental cliché, a trophy mistress in Caesar's Palace. Tellingly, the only significant *Cleopatras* of the post-*Gladiator* era are pornographic. Two thousand years on and Cleo is still a tacky nymphomaniac with too much mascara – straight out of Horace, Virgil and the rest of Octavian's propagandists. They wrote Greece out of her story; it complicated things inconveniently. For much the same reason, film-makers are in no hurry to put it back.

Rome, on the other hand, is instantly if misleadingly accessible. We feel that we have been there, in some ways all our lives. In the heyday of Roman epic films, merchandising tie-ins invited 1950s consumers to 'Make Like Nero' in *Quo Vadis* boxer shorts. Without any such prompting, their modern counterparts make like Augustus, re-founder of Rome, in the popular *Caesar* series of city-building simulation games. *Caesar*'s tag line – 'Build a City, Build an Empire' – encapsulates Rome's cinematic appeal. As befits a developed consumer culture, the range of choice is wide. We can imitate Julius Caesar, battlefield genius, in the real-time strategy games *Praetorians* or *Rome: Total War*. (The recent BBC series *Time*

Commanders allowed teams of work colleagues and fellow gym attendees to act out the same fantasy with an exhibitionist slant.) Or we can get under the skin of any Roman we can name and imagine in the online community of Nova Roma, a 'virtual nation' which plays Roman virtues surprisingly straight. Even Roman cooking is enjoying a belated (and admittedly minor) renaissance, making us quite literally consumers of Roman culture.

Making like Nero has obvious consumer appeal; making like Plato is a more daunting and less enticing prospect. It carries the threat of ideas, and ideas are much harder to sell. We fear that they will bore us (philosophy), corrupt us (Greek love) – or both. At its root, this half-realised jumble of ideas is Victorian. It brings us back to our starting-point of Plato; but we are now a long way from the Cave. Crusading apologists for love between men, most famously the aesthete and critic John Addington Symonds, found irresistible advantage in name-dropping the irreproachable founding father of philosophy at every turn; two of his most famous philosophical dialogues, *Phaedrus* and *Symposium*, take (one form of) male same-sex desire as a natural given. Symonds and his fellow late Victorian aesthetes capitalised on the shared classical education of a clubbish elite to retro-fit the *Symposium* with just the right flavour of elevating resonance; Greek love was, by inescapable tautology, synonymous with an eminently Victorian nobility of soul. That Greece was bourgeois humanity's indispensable model for excellence had, after all, been taken as read by everyone that mattered for a century or more. Symonds was one of the all-time great popularisers of Greek literature and thought; but his Greek love, veiled in learned euphemism, was coyly and unashamedly elitist. (His bridge-burning position statement *A Problem in Greek Ethics*, a foundational text of modern gay and lesbian studies, had an original print run of just ten copies.) Symonds and his coterie inadvertently helped poison the well of popular receptions of Greece generally – and of Plato in particular; generic multiplex anti-intellectualism finished the job. As Plato himself complained in his *Republic*, the audience doesn't want ideas; it wants spectacle, the bigger the better, and Greece has its work cut out to keep us entertained. Small wonder that So-crates jumps at Bill and Ted's once-in-a-lifetime invitation to 'party on, dude'. But how far will it take him?

2

MYTHCONCEPTIONS

From epic sagas to pint pots, the heroes of myth gave shape and sense to ancient Greek culture. Their exploits were tantalising reminders of a dimly glimpsed but glorious prehistory; their physiques thrillingly epitomised the values and aspirations of hard-edged Hellenic masculinity. They exported well, too: Roman culture snapped them up wholesale, internalising their values and passing them on in turn as icons of artistic machismo to the Renaissance and beyond. Why, then, have they not caught on as Hollywood legends? This chapter begins by exploring the representation in film of Hercules, the greatest mythical hero of them all – and the most adaptable. The Hercules of ancient myth and literature was an action hero and much, much more; his portfolio of personae ranged from philosophical poster boy to muscle-bound burlesque and outright slapstick. Whatever the intentions of individual auteurs, receptions of Hercules in film from the 1960s onwards have privileged high camp and the body beautiful over Stoic seriousness. Receptions in other media have recaptured some of the diversity of Hercules' ancient stories – and have delivered much better value for audiences. Why, then has this success not carried over to film? This chapter concludes by questioning whether the pumped-up and overexposed B-movie icon leaves contemporary cinema any room to manoeuvre in its attempts to re-muscle the *peplum* and make it competitive with Rome's action narratives. This question has particular and obvious relevance to Petersen's recent *Troy*, but a partial answer emerges only from context; and this context suggests a small and shrinking set of options, both for Greek myth and for the Greek (and ancient non-Roman) action hero generally.

This conclusion initially sounds unlikely. After all, Hercules is the only mythical Greek character to make a significant impact on modern popular culture. (His historical counterpart is Alexander the Great: ch.3 below.) Recent appearances have included a best-selling Disney animated film, a string of feature-length TV specials and the successful spin-off television series *Hercules: the Legendary Journeys*, which for a time could claim to be the most widely syndicated TV show on the planet. Hercules also made repeated cameo appearances in the spin-off's spin-off, the even more successful *Xena: Warrior Princess*. All of these recent outings have generated a substantial Herculean presence, not just on-screen but in related media and products: fans and consumers can buy into the Hercules franchise via novelisations, trading cards and much more. The cycle shows no sign of dying down; an entirely new Hercules TV franchise is in production. Yet some of the silences here speak volumes: where is Hylas, Hercules' fanciable teen sidekick? To find him we have to turn to the unauthorised narratives of fan activity, particularly **slash fiction**.

I write 'Hercules' and not 'Herakles' because everyone in the movies is going by a name not quite their own; cinema's use of Hercules has been arbitrary and opportunistic. Paradoxically, it closely resembles the development of his myth in antiquity. Stories belonging to local heroes – particularly the ancient-world musclemen of twentieth-century Italian cinema: Maciste, Ursus, Samson – are re-branded as Herculean for cosmopolitan anglophone consumption; or the heroes are fitted awkwardly into Hercules' family tree as hitherto unknown 'sons'. Similarly, Hercules himself appears in many unlikely supporting roles (e.g. as side-kick to Goliath, Samson or Odysseus) and in various improbable locations (Atlantis, Babylon, Rome; even, with Schwarzenegger, New York).

He journeys to the centre of the earth, fights kung-fu villains, fathers Roman gladiators. Hercules is an all-consuming myth – but also an endlessly fragmenting one.

Conversely, his spectacular success has necessarily entailed a general lack of development of other themes from Greek myth – a failure only accentuated by one-off curiosities like *Clash of the Titans* (1981). It is not just myth that suffers: Hercules' 1960s excesses continue to put a spanner in the works of straight-faced attempts to create new, big-budget *pepla* for the twenty-first century. This chapter will engage briefly with two heroic scenarios which at the time of writing appear permanently stuck in Development Hell: Vin Diesel's *Hannibal*, and the Thermopylae epic *Gates of Fire*. It will become evident that Herculean Muscle (with a cheerleading Hylas always lurking just out of shot) confounds all kinds of attempts to project a manly, macho 'Greece' for cinema audiences – and, as we'll see with *Hannibal*, extends to contaminate receptions of non-Roman antiquity generally. Other cultural products, too, are affected – at least to the extent that they follow film's lead. The medium that has now become such an indispensable driving force of the Holly-wood summer blockbuster – comics and graphic novels – provides a necessary frame of reference for understanding the rumoured new wave of muscleman epics. Graphic novels also supply an important test case: their narratives of Greek heroism stand or fall by their willingness to make a clean break with a worn-out cinematic tradi-tion. The often-despised pop-culture fodder of the comics industry increasingly informs cinema's own viewing constituency; a devil's advocate might argue that in ignoring it *Troy* loses any chance it had of developing a coherent and accessible vision of Greek antiq-uity. Instead, Petersen's film creates its own dead end via its fatally unreflective and genre-bound response to the classic problems we outlined in ch.1, unknowingly presenting itself as an overlong and irony-deficient *Legendary Journeys* or *Xena* episode.

Hercules in the Sahara

Las Vegas, 1954: the Sahara Hotel. Legendary agent and club owner Bill Miller, the man who discovered the Rat Pack and invented the lounge act, is giving Mae West her public back. They remember her for roles she played twenty years before – if they remember her at all; her runaway successes saved Paramount, but the studio has buried her films to appease the Production Code censors. Unable to make the projects she wanted, she ditched the studios in 1943 and went back to her vaudeville roots. Now 61, she'll end up touring for over a quarter of a century, packing out theatres and later promoting her autobiography. The Sahara is where it all starts coming together. The next year, Miller would move on to another hotel and launch the first of the Vegas 'feathershows', the high-gloss girly revues that would ultimately give us *Showgirls*. In the meantime, he showed Mae – and showed Mae boys …

The boys were bodybuilders, built to perfection – Reg Lewis, Mickey Hargitay, Gordon Mitchell, Dan Vadis. Up on stage with Mae at the Sahara, they showed off their physiques in classic poses and figure-hugging trunks. She sized them up as only Mae West could, with raised eyebrows, barbed witticisms and a song for the finale – 'I've got something for the girls: boys, boys, boys'. And all the boys were Hercules.

All were bodybuilders first and foremost, sportsmen. When they needed cash, they took part in photo shoots for physique magazines like *Strength and Health*; posing on a Vegas stage was hardly different. For most of them, the subsequent film appearances were just another profitable sideline. Mitchell went on to appear in over two hundred films, Vadis in two dozen; but Hargitay and Lewis were in only a handful. (Mitchell had a good day job already, too, as a schoolteacher.) To become a bodybuilder was already to emulate Hercules, within a discipline that had always consciously modeled itself on the hero's feats of strength. Recent scholarship by Maria Wyke has explored the development of muscleman culture via its magazine photo-features and advertisements, which promised insecure youngsters 'Herculean Muscle!'. The history of the sport was steeped in Herculean references. Charles Atlas, synonymous with the commercial cult of bulked muscle, named himself for Corman's hero, the sky-hefting Titan with whom Hercules once famously traded places. On stage in Vegas in 1954, the teenaged Reg Lewis was fresh from winning the Junior Mr Olympics award, named for an ancient athletic festival which Hercules famously founded. In 1960, Lewis became Mr Hercules – Mae presented the trophy; she'd kept in touch. He was still winning national competitions in his late forties. These men were serious in their commitment to the sport; and they were fresh, well-hung meat for the Italian production lines that fed America's B-movie cravings.

The Mae West Revue went on to sellout runs in New York and Atlantic City; but the boys went wherever a hero was needed, battling fire monsters, giant warriors and a Cyclops. 'Dan Vadis' (Constantine Daniel Vafiadis, an expatriate Shanghai Greek) ended up a Clint Eastwood regular, after a string of gladiator and Hercules movies in the 1960s. The Mae West Revue was his first taste of showbiz; he was only sixteen. His pal Mitchell was fifteen years his senior and just breaking into film; he made his mark as Herc-alike 'Atlas' in Italian sword-and-sandal B-movie *Atlas in the Land of the Cyclops* (1961), also found under the title *Maciste in the Land of the Cyclops*; and he played second fiddle to Gordon Scott's Hercules in *Hercules and the Princess of Troy* (1965), a.k.a. *Hercules vs. the Sea Monster*. Like Vadis, he is a familiar bit player from gladiator movies and westerns; but he also appeared in serious projects – among them *Fellini Satyricon* (1969). Lewis snagged the title role as 'Maxus', for what it was worth, in *Fire Monsters against the Son of Hercules* (1962), a.k.a. *Colossus of the Stone Age*, a.k.a. *Maciste contro i Monstri*.

'A.k.a.': everyone here is working under at least one pseudonym, players and parts alike. Lewis' 'Maxus' is a suspiciously Roman (or pseudo-Roman) moniker for a long-lost son of Greece's favourite hero, but he is by no means the strangest branch of the new Herculean family tree. The names and faces blur. Fellow strongman Richard Harrison, for instance, played two different 'Sons of Hercules' in two successive years – neither of them sons of Hercules. He was 'Glaucus' in *Messalina vs. the Son of Hercules* (1962), a.k.a. *L'Ultimo Gladiatore* – another Roman gladiator hero. And he was Perseus in *Perseus the Invincible* (1963), a.k.a ... etc. At least Perseus is a bona-fide Greek hero; but 1963 is a bit late for him to be joining the Hercules family tree.

Harrison had already starred in three Italian gladiator cheapies and would go on to more; he also appeared in a few spaghetti westerns; and later went into Hong Kong kung fu pictures. With his mixed baggage, Harrison is usefully representative of the classical muscleman phenomenon of the early to mid-1960s. His career shows how almost anything starring a hunk in trunks could be re-branded as 'Hercules and ...' for the American market. The (limited) recognition value of individual strongmen could help the transition, but only Steve Reeves came close to becoming a household name, and then only by virtue of having been in at the start; his cheap but effective *Hercules* and *Hercules Unchained* were the films that kick-started the trend. Instead, Hercules' own star image was the great enabler, sucking in other stories from far and wide. At a stretch, even Hong Kong chop-socky could go Herculean – *Hercules vs. Kung Fu* (of unknown date); its various listed titles include *Mr. Hercules against Karate*, blurring the already weak distinction between the ancient do-gooder and his modern emulators in competitive body-building. The films' marketers take advantage of Hercules' famous name (and throw in the occasional anachronistic brand-check of contemporary 'Herculean Muscle') to compensate for an ensemble of unknowns and a threadbare plot. The result is a patchwork body of newly dubbed Hercules films, stitched together bit by bit, after the fact – and out of decidedly mixed material.

To begin with, many of the ancient-world strongmen who become 'Hercules' via marketing start out as subjects of Rome, in keeping with the films' Italian origins. The names are a roll-call of patriotic Roman historiography, particularly Livy. As well as Richard Harrison's 'Glaucus', we have Steve Reeves – the classic sword-and-sandal Hercules – as a late-antique 'Emiliano' (Aemilianus) in a 1960 film, *Il Terrore dei Barbari*. Aemilianus never made it to the US drive-ins, where Italy's home-grown historical champions rang no bells; the dubbed version became *Goliath and the Barbarians*. In *La Regina delle Amazzoni* (1960), a duo of American strongmen (Rod Taylor and Ed Fury) are Roman heroes 'Pirro' and 'Glauco' (Pyrrhus and Glaucus). Confusingly, again, the dubbed version was released as *Colossus and the Amazon Queen* (plus two minor title variants). This was probably an attempt to cash in on the success of Sergio Leone's *The Colossus of Rhodes*; once again, names familiar to a chauvinistic Italian audience are immediately junked in favour of a generic muscleman identity.

Nowhere is this clearer – insofar as any part of this story can be clear – than with Italy's two great film musclemen, Ursus and Maciste. Ursus started life in Polish novelist Henryk Sienkiewicz' blockbuster serial novel of 1894-6, *Quo Vadis?*, soon adapted for the stage as a big-budget 'toga play' and now best known via Mervyn LeRoy's 1951 Technicolor version for MGM; the hero's 1960s players included bodybuilding champ Reg Park, a Yorkshire entrepreneur who also starred in successful Hercules films and later talked a young Arnold Schwarzenegger into trying for *Hercules in New York* (1980). Maciste, a gentle giant in the Ursus mould, was a home-grown hero who first appeared in Giovanni Pastrone's grandiose Carthage-bashing silent epic *Cabiria* (1914) and evolved into Italy's greatest sword-and-sandal hero. Ursus at least has the decency to sound classical; but the heroes are hard to sell to non-Italian audiences and are typically rebranded. Maciste becomes 'Atlas' in *Atlas against the Czar* (1963), trading on the name-recognition of Corman's *Atlas*; 'Colossus' in *Colossus and the Headhunters* (1962), cashing in again on Leone's *The Colossus of Rhodes*; 'Samson' in *Samson vs. the Giant King*; Hercules' son in *Triumph of the Son of Hercules* (1963); or Hercules himself in *Hercules of the Desert* (1964). The same actor, 'Kirk Morris' (a.k.a. Italian Adriano Bellini), plays Maciste in all five films – or rather four, since *Samson vs. the Giant King* is the same film as *Atlas against the Czar*.

And so it continues, through *Maciste in King Solomon's Mines* and every other unlikely title in the catalogue: Maciste, Maxus, Goliath, Poseidon, Son of Samson ... Often the names and the titles seem practically random, and there's nothing to be gained by reading too much into individual instances. The fickle impulses of distributors and dubbers, combined with the pile-'em-high economics of the drive-in circuit, drive a strikingly internationalist melting-pot of spur-of-the-moment identity tangles. Sometimes, revealingly, the name on the dubbed soundtrack is not the name on the poster. Any halfway classical-sounding name will do, once the audience has paid, even 'Maciste'; but one name in particular is guaranteed box-office. Hercules always pulls a crowd; and he covers for any number of distracting incongruities. Who cares that Ursus is played by Samson (muscular nonentity 'Samson Burke'), or Hercules by *Quo Vadis*-inspired Dan Vadis; or that *Samson vs. the Giant King* is also *Atlas against the Czar* and stars Maciste? Or, similarly, that *Samson and the Seven Miracles of the World* (1961) is also *Goliath and the Golden City*, was released in France as *Géant a la Cour de Kublai Khan*, and started life as *Maciste alla Corte del Gran Khan* ... Endlessly mutating, the sixties *pepla* are a film historian's despair.

Faking the Myth

The audience has paid for Hercules – *any* Hercules – and any wise-cracking strongman in a loincloth will do. But can he ever be the genuine article; or even get his story straight? The Italian strongman films give us a Hercules blurred and made indeterminate by multiple attributions and roles. He is not so much an identifiable hero as a collage, an improbable patchwork of borrowed and improvised tall tales; he doesn't add up. Paradoxically, his kitschy implausibility makes him an *authentic* Hercules – and so does our scepticism.

Ancient readers were already attuned to Herculean unreliability. There were simply so many stories; surely any one hero, even a supernatural strongman, couldn't have fitted them all in. Perhaps this is one reason that the *Legendary Journeys* franchise worked so well: he's a ready-made serial hero. In any case, not all of these stories agreed with one another. At least some of them had to be wrong and, from early on, Greek writers started picking holes in Hercules' CV. Hercules jumps ship from Jason's *Argo* when his young friend Hylas is kidnapped by nymphs; but Theocritus, a learned Hellenistic poet, digs up (or invents?) an alternative Argo story in which he hikes overland to catch up (*Idyll* 13). Theocritus insists that the mainstream version is a lie, no matter what the other heroes may have said. The Greek word for myth, *muthos*, means nothing more substantial than 'story'; any myth could be challenged. Even the basic chronology and motivation of Hercules' labours were open to question. Conventionally, Hercules is driven temporarily mad by Hera and kills his wife and children, undertaking the labours as a penance. However, Euripides' tragedy *Herakles* turns the story around: Hercules returns triumphant to his family, boasting of his famous labours; only then does Hera turn him into a murderer.

Greek theatre audiences accepted that some of the Herculeses doing the rounds in myth had to be spurious, too. We know of at least two ancient Greek comedies called *The Fake Hercules*; there may have been more. Even the genuine article was hardly a reliable source for his own adventures – assuming you could tell him apart from the wannabes. Old Comedy playwrights including Aristophanes wrote him up as a self-important, food-guzzling dimwit; and he became a loose prototype for the braggart soldier or *miles gloriosus* of New Comedy. Audiences also knew that he was vain; he liked to quote his own good reviews. In a papyrus fragment of a satyr-play by Sophocles he recites an approving quotation about himself from Pindar, the famous writer of victory odes.

In one fragment of an ancient Greek 'graphic novel' he goes further, actively faking his own legend. The cartoonist narrator mischievously asks Hercules to tell the story of his adventures, and the hero obligingly launches into a textbook account of his famous labours – a story familiar to his readers from great art and canonical literature. Meanwhile, satirical cartoons interrupt the flow of the text and show us a very different version of events, undercutting Hercules' versified 'press release'. A chubby Hercules bumps into the Stymphalian birds by accident while out fishing; later we seem to see him engaged in a much more photogenic labour, wrestling the legendary Nemean lion. But the picture is a posed shot, a fake – look closely and you can see that the 'lion' is just a statue (Fig. 5). The final surviving cartoon rejects the hero's dramatic reconstruction in favour of a fly-on-the-wall view of what actually happened. Hercules manfully chokes the life out of what the text slyly refers to as a 'lion-on-the-ground' – an inoffensive colour-changing lizard which the Greeks called *khamai-leon*. The painful puns and sight-gags of the cartoon Hercules papyrus suggest that, for at least some ancient readers, *any* Hercules was already a fraud and wannabe.

The 'hero roulette' of the Italian Hercules *pepla* picks up where the ancient sceptics leave off. The heroes shuffle a full deck of fake and seemingly interchangeable identities; the strongman actors

5. Hercules as heroic fake and inept self-publicist: the ancient
Oxyrhynchus papyrus.

who play them, too, tend to be working under assumed names.
False papers aside, the fake-Hercules plot continues to resurface,
as in *The Three Stooges Meet Hercules* (1962). Xena, too, must deal
with multiple imitators and wannabes. The persistence of this story
idea is unsurprising. Hercules' enthusiasm for rehearsing his own
myth at the drop of a hat is an authentically ancient feature – and
it authentically makes us suspect him of being inauthentic. Are we
being taken in by an exhibitionist fake claiming to be Hercules?
Then it *must* be Hercules … unless it's an exhibitionist fake.

Hercules in the Maze of the Minotaur (TV film, 1995)

Hercules runs into just this problem in the fifth of his 1990s films,
made by Universal for the US television networks and shot in New
Zealand. The hero, played by likeable hunk Kevin Sorbo, is en route
to the Minotaur's cave with his buddy Iolaus. Night is falling; they
find a tavern nearby, but none of the locals will believe Hercules'

story about the monster. Nor will they believe that he is Hercules. The innkeeper estimates that they see 'five or six' Hercules wannabes in an average week. Understandably so: as the voice-over to the opening credits proudly announces, even the genuine Hercules puts himself around a lot:

> No matter the obstacle, as long as there were people crying for help, there was one man who would never rest – Hercules.

Iolaus, who fancies himself the fast talker of the pair, is quick to produce proof that his Hercules is the genuine article: he repeats a story about one of their adventures, a fight with gravity-defying Amazons in animal masks. Iolaus' *muthos* is non-classical but we know that it's genuine within the modern canon of adventures established in the four earlier TV films: it's an extended flashback to *Hercules and the Amazon Women*. All the same, it sounds like an awfully tall tale, especially as Iolaus himself dies at the end of his own story – so how can he be telling it now? The innkeeper and her regulars are unconvinced.

Luckily for Hercules, a tavern brawl begins, allowing him to establish his hero credentials by beating up the sceptics. However, there's plenty to provoke scepticism in a modern TV audience – making the 1990s Hercules very much the genuine article. Made quickly and on the cheap, *Maze of the Minotaur* is heavily padded with long flashbacks to earlier exploits – seven in all – using footage culled from its four predecessors. The 1960s strongman pictures often resorted to the same money-saving dodge, an extreme example being *Maciste, Avenger of the Mayas*, which largely consists of footage from two movies with different leading men. The patchwork narrative of *Maze* also rips off an exploit that we know properly belongs to another famous hero, Theseus; and it mixes loose versions of known Herculean labours (the Hydra, again in extended flashback) with exploits that we know have been made up for previous movies (the giant 'Darga' and the Hercules-Zeus standoff on 'Mount Ethion'). Iolaus has even picked up some martial-arts skills during his recent travels in the East – allowing for a *Hercules vs. Kung Fu* reprise early in the movie, as he tries out his new moves on his old sparring partner.

Everything is here, very little of it makes sense, and none of it adds up: this is definitely Hercules. The contradictions and redundancies of the 'original' Hercules myths are recaptured by *Maze* and by the 1990s Hercules cycle which was to follow: the five TV movies spawned the more famous ongoing TV series, *Hercules: the Legendary Journeys*. In classical myth, for instance, Hercules' second wife is Deianeira. The TV films give us two Deianeiras, the first of whom is not married to Hercules at all. The second Deianeira is played by two actresses, who look quite unlike each other. The second actress to play this second Deianeira is killed by Hera – twice. Really, of course, Deianeira shouldn't die – it should be Megara, Hercules' first wife, and Hercules should kill her in a fit of madness. Then Deianeira should accidentally kill *him*. But who's counting? And all of this even before the first series has got under way ...

All of this is fun for classical *cognoscenti* and continuity buffs, but there are other, more glaring, discrepancies which are shared with *Legendary Journeys'* successful spin-off, *Xena: Warrior Princess*. For a Greek hero, Hercules spends a lot of time intervening in Roman narratives. The series' one-off characters have names chosen for their generic 'ancient' sound, many of them Roman or thereabouts. The first six episodes contain two fugitives from Virgil's *Aeneid* (Evander and Camilla), along with two Roman emperors slumming it in three walk-on plebeian roles (Marcus, Aurelius and Titus). Later episodes recycle these names for other one-off characters, and in Season 3 Hercules remarries a Romanesque 'Serena'. There are echoes here of Dan Vadis' Roman-blockbuster stage name. These Roman invasions penetrate deeper into the series' imaginative terrain. Episode

10, 'Gladiator', is a Roman gladiator epic in miniature – and full of conscious references to *Spartacus*. (Is this sixties *Hercules* Richard Harrison's gladiator-movie baggage, catching up with the franchise thirty years on?) The mythic framework of *Xena*, a wholly invented character, is if anything more solidly Greek than that of *Legendary Journeys*; in early episodes Xena helps Hercules free Prometheus, recaptures Sisyphus and is caught up in a war between Amazons and Centaurs. But this doesn't stop her bedding Julius Caesar in a Season 2 episode, 'Destiny', in which Xena also endures a Roman crucifixion. (Crucifixions return to derail another notionally Greek narrative in ch.3 below.)

But a Hercules who breaks across cultural boundaries and transforms into a Roman hero is *also* an authentic Hercules. The quintessential Hellenic hero only really comes into his own when he crosses over into his Roman 'afterlife'. The Romans took him up enthusiastically; like the modern film-makers, they found his myths wonderfully malleable. Modernity, in turn, takes its Hercules from Rome. Archaeology allows us to walk the streets of the unearthed town of Hercules – Roman Herculaneum, where (until Vesuvius) the hero brought fertility and good luck. In the well-known 'house of the Augustales' at Herculaneum, a sumptuous meeting-place for local officials of the imperial cult, the hero's labours and apotheosis are the subject of tasteful frescoes. Hercules' self-conscious readiness to toil for the world's good struck a chord with Roman ideas of Stoic duty to the State; they admired his stiff upper lip. In particular, his apotheosis might have helped the Augustales take on board the posthumous honours awarded to 'good' emperors in Augustus' new world order. Autocratic rule was no perk; it was a Herculean labour, willingly undertaken, and entitled its bearer to the same worship as Hercules once the burden was set aside in death. Later emperors were unwilling to wait that long to get the Hercules treatment. Commodus, the villain of *Gladiator*, notoriously modelled his personal style on that of Hercules. Official portrait busts showed him with a Greek-style beard and Hercules' classic accessories, the lion-skin and knotted club. He even hijacked a colossal statue of the sun-god Sol (erected as a self-portrait by Nero) to write his image large across Rome's skyline; the colossus was quickly modified into a gigantic Commodus in full Herculean drag. (Mussolini tried to resuscitate the idea two millennia on, but *his* sculptors never got further than casting one of his / Hercules' gigantic feet.)

Alarmingly, Hercules could be trouble for Romans, too. Marc Antony, avenger of Caesar and conqueror of the barbarous East, styled himself as Hercules on the coins he used to pay his troops; but his Hercules act was swiftly hijacked by his political rival, Caesar's nephew Octavian (later to repackage himself as Augustus). Octavian was able to point to areas of Antony's public image where Hercules was too close a comparison for comfort: his fondness for drink, and his voluntary enslavement to an exotic foreign queen. Hercules' comic episode as a cross-dressing maid to queen Omphale was a usefully suggestive parallel for Antony's entanglement with Cleopatra. Hercules was the great (new) Roman myth but he had too much baggage to be a safe propaganda tool; he could all too easily invite accusations of un-Roman activities, even of being a big sissy.

Modern treatments of Hercules suffer from a similar set of anxieties, but the focus has shifted. The hero's larger-than-life star image is what attracts film-makers; yet some of its most 'authentic' ingredients are still considered box-office death. We will see a similar pattern emerge for Alexander in the next chapter. Alexander, though, was a flesh-and-blood person before he became a myth. Perhaps misguidedly, we feel that we might discover true stories about him; and this opens up the possibility of dismissing other (inconvenient?) stories as lies. Any Alexander anecdote that threatens to frighten the horses can be argued away as a historical misunderstanding, as ancient or modern propaganda. With Hercules, nothing is true and the stories are everything. Some of the most important are about a boy called Hylas.

'Mommy, what's Daddy doing to Uncle Iolaus?': the sidekick problem

Hercules is frequently accompanied in his ancient adventures by a loyal young companion. 'Iolaus' is the son of the hero's half-brother, Iphicles, and accompanies Hercules on several adventures; 'Hylas' is a young favourite who sails with Hercules on the *Argo*. The two sidekicks are never in the same place at the same time; they are effectively interchangeable in modern versions, where their transliterated names even sound alike. (Just to muddy the waters further, one of Hercules' surviving sons is called 'Hyllus'; a semi-retired Iolaus teams up with him in Euripides' *Children of Herakles*, and Hyllus puts in an unexpected repeat appearance in the 1961 Reg Park *peplum*, *Hercules in the Haunted World*.)

Hylas in particular gets some readers hot under the collar. The ancient sources are unambiguous: Hylas is Hercules' jailbait boyfriend, his beautiful and self-regarding **eromenos**. Lust-struck water-nymphs kidnap and drown the boy, who has been sent off by the Argonauts to fetch water; Hercules, distraught, abandons the *Argo*'s mission to Colchis and wanders the countryside calling for his lost love. *Hercules: the Legendary Journeys* never re-created this episode, and its inclusion in any future version seems unlikely, but for ancient authors it was a favourite scene – Hercules at his most human, and Hylas' fifteen minutes of fame. Its most famous versions are Hellenistic, in Apollonius of Rhodes' new-model epic *Argonautica* and Theocritus' *Idylls*. For Theocritus, the story is well enough known to deserve a minor but crucial correction: as mentioned above, *his* Hercules gets over it, hiking overland to catch up with his fellow-Argonauts in time to complete the mission. The Roman poet Valerius Flaccus also produced an effective, neo-Homeric retelling in which Hercules' grief is as heroically unconstrained as Achilles' rage. Flaccus' version, too, takes the voyage of the *Argo* as its backdrop. Other versions clearly did the rounds. A papyrus fragment found a century ago in Egypt accidentally preserves part of a poetic catalogue of heroic man-boy relationships, with Hercules and Hylas playing a prominent role. It has been suggested that this list of examples (or *priamel*) was written to please Hadrian, justifying his relationship with his cute young boyfriend Antinous by digging up legendary precedents in the Greek literature that the Roman emperor loved so much. (Or is it just early Hercules slash?)

More modern receptions have had a trickier time justifying Hylas' inclusion. Don Chaffey's *Jason and the Argonauts* (1963) is usually remembered for Ray Harryhausen's splendidly scary skeleton warriors, but it makes bold choices in its portrayal of Hercules – most obviously in its intelligent against-type casting of British character actor Nigel Green, best known as the ramrod-straight drill sergeant in *Zulu* (1964). The screenplay, by Beverley Cross and veteran Jan Read, is a surprisingly literate and relatively faithful adaptation of Apollonius' Hellenistic epic. Cross and Read respect their source enough to include Hylas, but the film is at a loss to know what to do with him.

We shall see in ch.3 below that Greek historical films can have similar problems: in particular, what are they to do with Alexander the Great and *his* best buddy, Hephaestion? *Jason and the Argonauts* resembles Robert Rossen's 1956 *Alexander the Great* in contriving simultaneously to include and sideline the problem character. Partly this is achieved at the level of casting, as in Rossen's picture. Hercules in *Jason* is a heavy hitter with stage experience; Hylas is John Cairney, a minor Glaswegian bit-player. Partly, too, the film pushes Hylas to the margins by minimising his role in the action and removing his motivation as a character. The kid sidekick is welcomed on board, not as Hercules' squeeze, but as a plucky trickster who'll be an asset to the expedition (an un-classical characterisation established in a pre-voyage scene involving a discus). But the script denies him any opportunity to display these positive traits, and gets him out of the way as quickly as possible. Even the nymphs are written out in case they remind us of Hylas' 'sissy' narcissism. The clear implication of the ancient sources is that Hylas sets himself up for a fall: he's too in love with his own good looks to just fill the jug and go without lingering to check out his reflection. Instead, *Jason and the Argonauts* squashes him under the feet of Harryhausen's giant bronze robot, Talos. Nigel Green's Hercules is badly shaken, and leaves the ship's company just as in Apollonius; but it's no longer at all clear *why* – other than professional embarrassment at his failure to manage a promising protégé.

A recent made-for-TV *Jason and the Argonauts* (2000) reprises the 1963 storyline on the cheap; most of the characters and incidents stay in, but Hylas' role is cut altogether in favour of a strictly heterosexual quest. Jolene Blaylock, now better known as Vulcan science officer T'Pol in the *Star Trek* prequel series *Enterprise*, plays Jason's love interest Medea; Dennis Hopper and Derek Jacobi slum it in cameo roles. The 2000 TV special is a notoriously feeble version of the story, but its decision to leave Hylas on the cutting-room floor makes sound economic sense. Character in cinema is best defined by actions, and a passionate kiss between Hercules and Hylas is an action too far for all but the boldest production companies. Several of the *Alexander* contenders peddled an openly bisexual conqueror in their pre-production publicity, and aspects of this persona filtered through into Stone's final cut; but this is a very different game: on this, see ch.3 below.

Legendary Journeys, too, prudently skirted around Hercules' penchant for Boy Wonders – but it did so by building the character up, not by cutting it altogether. The series' sidekick, Iolaus, is very much a youngish grown-up who can usually take care of himself – and occasionally has to step in to save Hercules' skin. The *Hercules* series is action-packed but also character-driven, and it invests heavily in Iolaus' development as a stand-alone character. He has motives, muscles, a distinctive fighting style and a personality that evolves as the series progresses. He is a much better effort than the Hylas of *Jason and the Argonauts* – or, really, the pin-up Hylas of Apollonius' *Argonautica*. Even so, bits of Hylas leak through into Iolaus at moments of heroic bonding. In *Maze of the Minotaur*, Hercules and Iolaus have settled down as farmers after their previous adventures; both are bored silly, and any excuse for an adventure will do. (Their motivation thus uncannily mirrors that of the TV movie's producers.) Iolaus drops in on his pal to reminisce about the good old days, and brags about his subsequent travels in the East; one thing leads to another. Deianeira and the children walk into the barn to find the pair in tight leather trousers, stripped to the waist and entwined in what they assure her is a wrestling move:

> *small child*: Mommy, what's Daddy doing to Uncle Iolaus?
> *Deianeira*: I don't know, sweetie, I was wondering the same thing myself.

And so were we ... But once the ongoing series got its act together, it was consistently careful to avoid camping up the relationship between Hercules and Iolaus. On this point, *Hercules: the Legendary Journeys* stands in stark opposition to its successful spin-off, *Xena: Warrior Princess*. Although constrained by what the networks would stand for, *Xena* consciously courted a lesbian audience via increasingly heavy hints –most famously in the episode 'A Day in the Life' – about the relationship between the heroine and her sidekick, Gabrielle. Audiences responded enthusiastically to this erotically charged subtext. The implicit romantic tension clearly helped the show expand its market share, broadening its appeal beyond the obvious, and still indispensable, core demographic of teenaged boys. (The TV series *Buffy: the Vampire Slayer* enjoyed a similar mid-run rejuvenation when it brought Buffy's best friend, Willow, out of the closet.) Receptions of the show in unofficial media, too, embraced the idea of a hidden relationship between Xena and Gabrielle. It became a favourite topic for female-authored slash fiction online. Meanwhile, a string of 'unauthorised' episode guides and series companions titillated the guys by cataloguing the show's double-entendres and smouldering glances.

None of this fan activity transferred back to the original *Legendary Journeys*, which shared *Xena*'s commercially essential core audience of male adolescents. The scriptwriters' assumption – almost certainly correct – was that this audience would find *Xena*'s hinted lesbianism alluring but would switch channels at any suggestion of a gay leading man. Accordingly, they were consistently careful to keep the show on the straight and narrow (thus nipping in the bud any potential gay receptions). Episode guides and other spin-offs play along, reinforcing the heroes' straight personae. Hercules' original mythology is discussed at length, but selectively: Hylas is conspicuous by his absence. Hercules and Iolaus are doomed to be just good friends.

Serial infidelity

Is Hercules himself, though, any less of an intractable absence? Is there anything behind the chiseled good looks and the 'Herculean Muscle'?

Often, of course, Hercules isn't himself (or is only himself as a marketing afterthought): he is Maciste, Ursus, Colossus, Géant, or a variety of 'Sons of …'. To be a proper Hercules, he must be inauthentic often enough – unfaithful to, or implausible in rehearsing, his own myth. This Hercules is the perfect post-modern hero; the simulacrum is everything. The Hercules of the twentieth and early twenty-first centuries, self-consciously photogenic, has pulled it off with panache. He has also revealed a strong sense of humour, knowingly resuming his ancient role as class clown. It is probably no accident that the most 'unfaithful' Hercules of all, trouser-clad WWE-alike Kevin Sorbo, has been far and away the most satisfying – and a runaway commercial success. *Hercules: the Legendary Journeys'* multiple infidelity to classical sources was if anything its greatest strength. Any Hercules story is always already a series of citations – conscious or unconscious recyclings of previous versions, along with incorporations of 'new' material – and *Maze of the Minotaur* and its companion pieces are the perfect exemplars of this very ancient trend. (The twelve labours, as featured on the sculpted metopes of the ancient Temple of Olympian Zeus, were already an improvised and spin-doctored 'greatest hits' collection.) Sincerely tongue-in-cheek, *Legendary Journeys* and *Xena* were worthy successors to the Herculean excesses of the sixties *pepla*. They represent the latest growth spurt of a Hydra-headed monster that has swallowed the myths of other Greek heroes and continues to gorge on everything from gladiators to kung fu. The ancient Hercules franchise has been rejuvenated, pretty much literally. A *Young Hercules* was spun off early on; and a new and entirely unconnected *Hercules* series is set to appear shortly, this time with a strong youth emphasis.

By a combination of attrition and absorption, Hercules has come to stand as the paradigmatic hero of Greek myth; but he has also come a long way from Greece. He began the journey in antiquity, when Rome bought out his contract; the Italian muscleman flicks of the 1960s assert an unbroken and long-standing Roman stake in the hero's management. Meanwhile, America beckons; the Italian strongmen brush up their CVs, recasting their stories and identities for an easier assimilation into the new Rome beyond the

Pillars of Hercules; and the hero's old story of westward migration resumes in response to a new cultural imperialism. Does Hercules labour only for non-Greeks? While the Italian musclemen oiled up as 'Herculean Muscle' at the drive-in, modern Greece high-mindedly stayed away from the meat market: its contemporary forays into classical myth were limited to the High Culture cul-de-sac of reverential communion with long-dead classical tragedians. The latter-day Greek nation's relationship to its classical namesake has always been a difficult one to negotiate, both internally and in the eyes of a wider European and global culture. The flipside of the West's philhellenic nostalgia for the ancient cradle of democracy has been a consistent tendency to regard contemporary Greece with dismissive condescension as a fruit fallen far from the tree of the Tradition. Perhaps inevitably, Greek culture's receptions of its self-declared autochthonous legacy have been conservative and risk-averse. An insistence on dramatic authenticity and serious values has left Hercules – braggart, clown, and heroic serial faker – out of work. At the beginning of the twenty-first century, non-Greeks everywhere know his name; Disney and Kevin Sorbo have made him the world's hero. In Greece, meanwhile, he is little more than a brand of cement.

Barbarians at the Gates

If Hercules, its acknowledged paradigmatic hero, has sold out, then what hope for Greek myth as a whole? What hope, too, for the second-string action heroes of ancient Greek culture, whether mythical or merely real? This chapter concludes by engaging with the obvious culprit in recent attempts to film Greek myth, Wolfgang Petersen's lamentable *Troy*; but first it sketches out a context that set *Troy* up for failure. We will look into two long-touted film narratives which are currently going nowhere, for reasons that have a lot to do with Hercules' overload of 1960s labours. The sniffy reviews and poor takings of *Troy* and *Alexander* aren't helping their case; but these projects were already circling the drain, and their chances now appear vanishingly slim. The obstacles they ran up against – axe-grinding advocacy groups, casting headaches, king-sized egos, source problems, and, above all, the sheer unwanted weight of inconvenient past receptions – nicely set up the issues for my final major chapter on the many and varied modern attempts to film Alexander the Great. Each of the projects under analysis here aimed to win critical acclaim and financial success by reuniting the Herculean bodybuilding ideal with popular culture's idea of 'Greece' – or, at least, divorcing it from the hunky gladiators of 'Rome'. Charles Atlas-like, they undertook to make non-Roman antiquity manly again. Yet just as with Hercules, Rome kept straying into shot; and Hylas was never far out of frame. Could alternative media and subcultural receptions offer a way forward?

Vin Diesel, *Hannibal* (pre-production)

To begin with a non-Greek muscleman may initially seem perverse, but the moral panic focalized by Vin Diesel's unrealised Carthaginian epic *Hannibal* – a panic essentially predicated on receptions of sixties *pepla* – lends crucial perspective to a slew of going-nowhere receptions of non-Roman antiquity in the 1990s and 2000s. This may be all it ever does: I for one would love to see this film, but Diesel's passionate commitment to the project has not yet moved it beyond pre-production. (The star of *XXX* and *The Fast and the Furious* is also keen to direct and produce.) Why not? At a more advanced stage, it wouldn't have helped that Stone's plodding *Alexander* had anticipated *Hannibal*'s selling point; war-elephants now looked like last year's gimmick. And the usual difficulties of representation – what does the ancient world look like, if not Rome? – would have been as acute here as they ever could be. Famously, Rome wiped Carthaginian culture off the map; there's nothing left for a filmed Carthage to look like, or certainly nothing a modern audience will recognise. The script, by *Gladiator*'s David Franzoni, similarly might not have helped *Hannibal* stake out a culturally distinctive position. None of these objections, however, even got a look-in. Herculean Muscle, filtered via the Roman arena, was the only factor that really counted in setting up *Hannibal* as a non-starter for its prospective consumers. Critics and fans alike used Diesel-as-Hannibal to talk up the prospect of non-Roman ancient muscle as inherently problematic, with star image a very significant additional complication. Online advocacy unwittingly but unerringly set up Diesel as a latter-day Roman superstar gladiator – hulking, pumped-up totty with the cheap sexual allure that comes with casual violence. Diesel was reviled as a washed-up, ex-porn actor, too dim even to dump his old screen name; many comments also carried a distinct homophobic edge. This word-of-mouth smear campaign of *ad hominem* fabrication amounted to actual slander and little trace of its passing now survives; the surviving *Hannibal* discussion threads on the Internet Movie Database (IMDb) are a tattered web due to the unprecedented number of postings which were promptly deleted by a responsibly minded site management. Yet in an industry where word of mouth is everything, these transient Chinese Whispers were perhaps enough to derail *Hannibal*'s sales pitch.

The startling vehemence of fan and critical reactions to even the remote prospect of Diesel-as-Hannibal – crucially, not to Diesel *or* to Hannibal *per se* – is revealing, and sets up many of the concerns we will address in the next chapter's analysis of the *Alexander* phenomenon. In *Hannibal*'s case at least, the reaction is essentially a residual outcome of Hercules' 1960s overexposure – overexposure in every sense, and very often in the anomalous setting of the Roman gladiatorial arena. Under Roman law, gladiators were disqualified from public speech in forum and law-court, just like prostitutes and for much the same reasons; it was unthinkable that they should claim a stake in the family values of the Roman body politic. The term for their disqualification was *infamia*, 'infamy'. The *Hannibal* backlash unknowingly resurrects *infamia* as – so far – a one-off ban. Diesel's thrillingly muscular physicality, the attribute that makes him such a strong contender for the role of Hannibal, becomes instead the fatal flaw that disqualifies him from articulating his vision as director-producer-(porn)star – and that confirms his improper qualifications, his insurmountable inauthenticity, his fish-out-of-water status as historical film-maker. We will see further examples of this kind of backlash, again predicated on star image and directorial posturing, in the next chapter. (One figure common to both narratives is *Gladiator* director Ridley Scott, who was talking up *Hannibal* to no effect at about the same time as he was peddling his similarly never-made *Alexander*.) In the case of *Hannibal*, the mere fact that the prospective star is well-built – and that his character's back-story isn't Roman – is enough to precipitate backlash. Diesel's Hannibal presents a threatening prospective **Other** to Hollywood's safely heterosexualised muscular Romans. Their rising hemlines and calculated meat-market appeal are pervasively and insistently coun-terbalanced by sound family-man credentials. As we saw in ch.1, toga spectaculars from the Victorian era to the present day have ritualistically recycled the same old plot: virile, jaded but redeem-able pagan boy meets pious, distant but attainable Christian girl and sparks fly. With his nods towards the nineties new man, *Gladiator*'s conveniently widowed Maximus is a minimal update of this time-worn, romantic-tension-by-numbers routine. (The Christians ended up on the cutting-room floor, but only just.) This commercially proven formula reliably shifts product via the established toga-epic associations we saw in ch.1 above: action, sports, romance. These themes sell Rome on film, and simultaneously, via Rome, any of a range of leisure and lifestyle consumables: celebrity sex, soccer, soft drinks (Fig. 6). However, the formula refuses to transfer straightforwardly to ancient non-Roman scenarios. Consequently, Diesel's project was instantly trivialised in public discourse as no more than a latter-day Hercules *peplum*, with all the usual nudge-wink subtexts in tow. (As Mae put it: 'Boys, boys, boys …') There's an edge here, too, of racism in response to Diesel's mixed Mediterranean ethnicity, a blend ideally suited to Phoenician / African Hannibal (a rival project was to have starred a too-old Denzel Washington) but less so to the tried-and-tested toga formula that, in *Gladiator* as elsewhere, consigns non-white characters to the role of faithful sidekick. *Hannibal's* premise of opposition to and refusal to subordinate itself to 'Rome' denied its hero / star the possibility of redemptive Anglo-Saxon ruggedness and invited a minor moral panic – a toga'd-up thumbs down from the pundits. Diesel's universally derided sub-*Kindergarten Cop* comedy *The Pacifier* (2005) was probably the final nail in *Hannibal's* coffin – but by then it hardly needed one. Fan and critical discourse had written it off, sight unseen.

Dining in Development Hell: *Gates of Fire* and Miller's *300*

Taking its provisional title and storyline from Steven Pressfield's well regarded historical novel, *Gates of Fire* was one of at least two recently announced films of the battle of Thermopylae, where 300 Spartans and assorted allies made a heroically doomed stand against the juggernaut of Xerxes' imperial Persian armies. A rival studio, Fox, was also for a time talking up a prospective remake of their solid 1962 property, the actioner-*cum*-romance *300 Spartans*. Both projects sought to sell themselves off the ancient-warfare excitement of *Gladiator*. Advance publicity (as always, so much hot air until someone starts nailing a set together) played up the projects' rough-hewn macho credentials, hinting at Bruce Willis and

6. Action, sports, romance: soft drinks and soccer heroics sell each other via the still-potent image of Roman gladiator machismo. The sales pitch refuses to transfer to Greek action heroes.

George Clooney as potentials for the role of Sparta's warrior king, Leonidas. Again, though, just as with *Hannibal*, the studios' attempts to talk up their as yet nonexistent projects cut both ways. Word-of-mouth and online speculation were working against Thermopylae's prospects right from the start – and often without meaning to.

The problem this time wasn't so much star image as the dead weight of previous receptions. Foremost among these was 300, a 1998 graphic novel by veteran US comics auteur Frank Miller. Inspired by the square-jawed heroics of the old 300 *Spartans* movie, this pivotal retelling found itself endlessly cited by fans and critics as a paradigmatic model and central point of reference for any discussion of *Gates of Fire*, other Thermopylae projects and Greek action heroics generally. Since the late 1980s and *Batman*, American superhero comics have become increasingly central to Hollywood's summer blockbuster production line. This trend is only partly explained by the enticing prospect of predictable box-office and never-ending franchises, although the decades-long back-story of *X-Men*, for example, guaranteed healthy ticket sales to generations of nostalgic devotees. More widely, and moving beyond the super-hero genre, Hollywood has demonstrated an increasing dependence on comics and the new graphic novels for fresh writing talent, storylines and techniques. This trend reflects a nineties New Wave of mainly British writers whose literate and complex narratives reinvigorated the US comics industry.

Marketed as a prestige product, 300 is self-consciously upmarket in its production and design values and literary ambitions. It was initially released as a series of five comics; the publishers ambitiously promoted these as 'chapters'. Even the paper stock is thick and lustrous. The opening pages are beautiful in their lack of economy: in all, twenty uninterrupted double-page spreads or 'splashes'. Most comics cram multiple panels onto each page – more story for the money – but Miller makes each of his opening pages into half of a single huge panel, a showcase for his cinematic sensibilities and sparse dialogue. The subcultural medium of the comic (here insistently 'graphic novel') is redeemed as highbrow Art, or, more particularly, as Cinema. Explicitly inspired by *300 Spartans*, *300* is not so much a comic as a film remake by other means – widescreen format and all. The standard gestures towards authenticity are all here: the naming of sources, the attempts at authentic mise-en-scène. Miller's Spartans fight in an approximation of a phalanx and groom their long hair in the lulls between battles. The authenticity ends there, although the fun is only just beginning. The Spartans bound through *300* in uniform Technicolor-scarlet cloaks left over from a toga epic, a superhero comic – or both. Legionary-style red cloaks were a problem in *The Colossus of Rhodes* (Fig. 4); here, the problem is compounded by the additional baggage of the comics medium and by Miller's own star image as the auteur who re-invented superhero comics with *The Dark Knight Returns*. The Spartans are simultaneously an ersatz super-team – their uniform bronze shields carry a stylised Greek *lambda* ('L'), anticipating the X of X-Men – and wannabe Roman legionaries. Miller's self-conscious citations of his earlier artwork (for instance, Xerxes' elite Immortals are stylised ninjas, transposed from his *Elektra* series) reinforce the Spartan superhero identity. In turn, *300*'s iconography is folded back into the superhero genre in Miller's recent return to the Batman mythos, *DK2: the Dark Knight Strikes Again*. Leonidas' Spartan queen is recycled as Diana, queen of the Amazons – better known to most readers as Wonder Woman.

Caught between the baggage of two conservative genres – ancient-world epic and superhero comic – *300* founders in classic *peplum* style, and all the usual subtexts come bubbling through. The L-Men work out in fetishistic leather gear ('Are you liking this, Spartan?' 'I'm loving it, sir!': Fig. 7); nor has Miller realised that his *lambda* logo is shared with a number of prominent queer rights groups,

7. 'I'm loving it, sir!' (300) – flexing that Herculean muscle.

including, as it happens, a gay and lesbian classical caucus. Writing
300 as a *peplum* drags in the high camp, in spite of an explicitly
conservative presentist agenda which posits freedom-loving Greece
as a prototype USA and hawkish Sparta as its citizen militia.

Miller is not the first comics writer to latch onto Sparta's brand-
name recognition in modern popular culture. The city's soundbite
reputation for gritty, tight-lipped heroics ('Spartan', 'Laconic') prom-
ises to match the medium's costumed superheroes thrill for thrill
– the last, best hope for a heterosexually presentable Greece. Deference to cinematic precedent, however, derails attempts to carve out
a toga-free narrative. Frank Bellamy's cult sixties *Eagle* strip *Heros
the Spartan* is a case in point: the title character is Spartan-born,
but the story keeps him well away from insidious Greece. Taking its
cue from the recent hit movie *Spartacus* (1960), *Heros* folds Sparta
into the Roman history suggested by its sound-alike. Its protagonist
has been raised as the adoptive son of a Roman general and is now
a soldier in Rome's legions – complete with red legionary cloak, of
course, just like Miller's Leonidas and for the same contradictory
reasons.

More broadly, in film and (seemingly) other popular media too,
modern receptions of manly Sparta can never escape the legacy of
commie / queer baggage trailed by its near-namesake. Spartacus is
not just the hero of a famously camp toga epic, recently renewed
as a classic queer text by the restoration of its infamous 'oysters
and snails' scene; he is a pervasive gay icon, of which the annual
Spartacus Gay Guides are perhaps the best known of countless
commercial manifestations. And Spartacus is also a hero of the
workers' revolution, the figurehead of Rosa Luxemburg's Spartacist
movement and an icon of resistance for Howard Fast, *Spartacus'*
communist author.

Popular culture has a hard time keeping its Spartans and Sparta-
cuses apart. *Spartacus* (1960) sneaked Greek love into the Roman

war machine; *Heros the Spartan*, 300 and the Spartacus Gay Guides keep things good and confused. Popular culture's militarised Sparta is a self-contradictory mess, inevitably filtered through both Roman mise-en-scène and, simultaneously, sixties camp nostalgia – a filter now heavily overlaid with the brighter colours of Spartacus' explicitly queer receptions. Straightening out the Spartans is a Herculean undertaking. *Gates of Fire*, Steven Pressfield's fine and bloody novel of Thermopylae and the official 'source' of the would-be epic film, came out in the same year as 300 and shares the comic's urge to reinstate the Three Hundred as icons of democratic machismo. Like Pressfield, Miller intends his hard-bodied Spartans as a re-muscling of the *peplum* to match the gritty heroics of Ridley Scott's *Gladiator* (2000), a conservative retort to the queers and commies ('Persians! Come and get it') – but Miller can't keep a good subtext down. His constant watchword is 'freedom', whether in rightist politics or authorial autonomy (Miller is laudably active in industry anti-censorship lobbying); but his aspirational counterfeiting of cinema's Greece leaves his narrative remarkably *un*free.

The new fan and critical Thermopylae-discourse ostentatiously bought into Miller's vision. Name-dropped repeatedly in fan and critical discourse as a defining modern treatment which any future Greek heroic epic would have to meet head-on, 300 queered the pitch for *Gates of Fire* and other projects too. Subsequently, of course, it would head them off at the pass. But Thermopylae remains a resonant story, bigger than any one telling; and 300 was still very much a one-off within an American comics industry that generally avoids ideas-heavy Greece. Its attempt to manoeuvre its hoplites into graphic-novel hegemony came at a heavy price – and left Greece as peripheral to the industry's concerns as it had always been, New Wave or no New Wave.

Troy, Troy Again

An outstanding exception, and a striking counter to 300's wide-screen narrowness, is *Age of Bronze*, Eric Shanower's cult re-telling of the Trojan War on an epic scale – and a shoestring (www.age-of-bronze.com). The story is as faithful to the archaeological and literary sources as Shanower can make it; but it is also beautifully written and drawn, and an award-winning favourite among fellow comics professionals. Nonetheless, *Age of Bronze* retains a defiantly small-press ethos which cuts against the promotional priorities of a publishing and retail industry fixated on pushing brightly-coloured superheroics (300, ultimately, included) to a primarily adolescent readership. In particular, *Age*'s openly gay reading of the relationship between Achilles and Patroclus – deftly handled and, of course, faithful to ancient Greek receptions of Homer – was nicely timed to inject controversy into the media circus of *Troy*. Issue #14 (August 2002) delivered the long-foreshadowed first kiss, an affirmation of *Age*'s outsider status within an industry that is itself still relatively marginal to the mainstream, albeit increasingly indispensable to the Hollywood production line. Wolfgang Petersen's *Troy* went out of its way to avoid this storyline; advance publicity accentuated the heterosexual romance between Paris and Helen through over-reporting of the casting process, and Patroclus was clumsily rewritten as Achilles' 'cousin'. Nonetheless, this left-field and infinitely more nuanced narrative (Fig. 8) grabbed its own small slice of popular *Troy*-discourse, in part via tie-in TV reporting of the new excavations at Troy / Hisarlik; a widely syndicated Discovery Channel documentary made extensive and striking use of Shanower's distinctive visual style in animated form, re-fleshing the dry archaeology far more evocatively (not to mention cheaply) than Petersen's overblown epic. Big-budget cinema could struggle all it liked to keep Achilles in the closet; but the products and activities of subculture conspired to keep the closet door wide open for audiences and mainstream media alike.

Troy (2004)

Sword drawn, eyes narrowed for the kill, Achilles sprang catlike across the pedestrian precinct.

The poster, a holographic design, was an expensive gimmick; but it undeniably did its job in drawing the attention of passing shoppers to Petersen's hotly tipped *Iliad*-based epic. Brad Pitt's buffed and toned Achilles flexed his (Herculean?) muscle in city centres nationwide. One mighty leap (albeit a jerkily animated one) promised adventure, sports, romance – all of Hollywood's blue-chip sales pitches rolled into one heroic physique. At the same time, the dynamism of the promotional materials promised the aggressive reclamation – even the re-conquest – of a Hollywood genre once thought moribund. Had Petersen brought the *peplum* back to vigorous, leonine life?

If so, alas, he had done so only by turning the *peplum* into an ersatz toga – at least by the time the marketing department was done. Adventure, sports, romance: these are the familiar sales pitches, not just of action films generally, but specifically of the Roman epics of the fifties. (Maria Wyke's *Projecting the Past*, cited in the 'Further Reading' section at the end of the book, gives an excellent account of these extra-cinematic considerations.) *Troy* was already underselling itself as more of the same old thing: a Roman epic manqué. At the same time, though, the poster assumed too much. Potential buyers of the *Troy* experience were tacitly compelled to approach the product from a particular angle – in the case of the poster, quite literally. If you came at it from the narrowly prescribed 'correct' angle of stage left, a jerky narrative sense and direction emerged; but passers-by who failed to play along with the poster's

8. As not seen in *Troy*: subcultural receptions can be at once more 'authentic' *and* more groundbreaking.

implicit agenda instead watched holographic Achilles take a mighty, juddering leap backwards. The symbolic irony of this moment would become all too apparent when they saw the actual film.

Petersen's film, pitched in the wake of *Gladiator* as a new beginning for classical epic, played out much like its poster: a moderately successful gimmick, but ultimately not nearly as clever as it thought it was; and in some ways a big step back from the more adventurous receptions of ancient Greece that were beginning to emerge elsewhere in popular culture at around the same time. For classicists, the most obvious gripe is that the film is unfaithful to its notional source, Homer's *Iliad*: Homer's gods are kept off-screen (hardly a mistake in cinematic terms) and the plot is out to lunch. The same classicists will concede immediately and with good humour that the ancient Greeks remodelled Homer's narratives all the time, most famously to make good plots for tragedies, and that most of the Trojan War isn't even in Homer to begin with. Instead the broad bones of the traditional version derive from a slew of second-string epics known to us only via fragments and citations, the so-called Epic Cycle. Many of the changes, too, are very entertaining for the *cognoscenti*. Hector kills Menelaus, Briseis kills Agamemnon, Iphigeneia is sacrificed to running-time on the cutting-room floor, Andromache and Astyanax escape through the secret passage (*sic*); so much for Homer, the Cycle, Aeschylus' *Oresteia* and most of Euripides' war plays. At least Odysseus is left alive at the end of the picture, although the prospects of an *Odyssey*-based sequel must be slim. But this is nitpicking (of a kind at which classicists notoriously excel).

At times, too, the film nods to Homer with something approaching charm. Achilles, scowling at Agamemnon, slings shame-culture invective in self-consciously Iliadic style: 'You sack of wine!' The imagery of Homer's famous extended similes, particularly wild nature, filters through into the film's mise-en-scène and dialogue. A predatory

Achilles urges on his black-clad Myrmidons by hailing them as 'lions'; and Hector is seen on the voyage home from Sparta carving a small wooden lion as a toy for his infant son Astyanax. Once war is joined, Hector 'Tamer of Horses' (his stock Homeric epithet) rides to battle as a cavalry commander, sporting a good approximation of the horse-hair plume he wears in the *Iliad*. Many individual scenes carry across, albeit with altered emphases. Homer's famous *teikhoskopia* – the episode in *Iliad* 3 where Priam, on Troy's walls, invites Helen to identify to him the chieftains of the Achaean army – makes it into the picture, more or less, as does the classic scene of the ransoming of Hector's body (when Priam's appalling, rat-like teeth carry much of the pathos of the moment).

For the rest, *Troy* throws the bard out with the bathwater. Although Petersen sensibly backs away from Homer's divine apparatus, he half-heartedly keeps the Greek gods in the cultural frame – though in his version only the non-Greek Trojans respect them. Classicists might hope that this is meant as Euripidean tragic pessimism (Euripides' war plays are bitterly cynical about religious pretexts for atrocity) but it reads on-screen as a sop to outdated narrative conventions; Petersen's disbelieving Greeks are a watered-down version of the cynical Roman pagans of those same old fifties toga epics. In fact the cliché of pagans who cannot muster belief in their many gods goes back to the Victorian blockbuster novels and stage melodramas about the persecuted early Church on which Hollywood's Cold War Romes (and, earlier, the epics of the silent twenties and talkative thirties) were indirectly based. Petersen's backwards leap is greater than he realises and ties him into traditions of Roman reception rather than Greek.

More generally, there are basic failures of motivation and coherence. *Troy*'s dialogue goes a long way towards engaging with the value-system of Homer's heroes – Achilles and Agamemnon in particular talk a good game on shame, loot and posterity – but

Hollywood narrative conventions keep it hot air. Homeric heroes rob their fallen foes to assert and enhance their own glory; Hollywood heroism, answering to modern Western values, is more constrained. Central to the industry's version of heroism is the idea of the *romantic* hero, the 'male lead'. We have seen how the fifties version of Homer's story, *Helen of Troy*, ran into difficulties in its attempt to turn Paris (Western literature's first truly smackable antihero) into a square-jawed and straight-shooting romantic lead; a recent and identically titled TV version (2003), timed to cash in on *Troy*'s publicity, went the same route with not much more success. *Troy* tries something different. Commendably, and thanks in part to some apt casting, it gives us an authentically 'Homeric' Paris – a callow, shallow pinup and poseur. (Diane Kruger's otherwise pretty dull, platinum-blonde Helen has the measure of him: 'You are very young, my love'.) But, disastrously, it displaces the 'male lead' role onto Achilles. Petersen's story turns him into a romantic prototype for Hollywood's Robin Hood; he sneaks into Troy in the wooden horse and climbs the walls of Nottingham castle (the citadel of Troy) on a solo mission to rescue Maid Marian (Briseis) from the wicked Sheriff of Nottingham (Agamemnon). The literal horseplay of the final reel signals *Troy*'s final descent into genre-confused bathos; we expect Xena, Warrior Princess to show up at any moment. Indeed, in *Xena*'s own cheekily revisionist Girl Power version, Xena and Helen stow away in the horse and make a clean getaway, rolling out of the burning city towards new adventures.

Certainly Xena would feel pretty much at home in *Troy*. This is surely the last thing the production designers intended; but the film's insistently 'ethnic', Pacific rim-orientated mise-en-scène makes the comparison inevitable. The Trojan elite (or what's left of them – to avoid confusing the viewers, Priam's fifty sons are whittled down to two) parade in tie-dyed sarongs and wraps. (One reviewer sniped that Hector's shipboard togs 'seem to have been stitched together from batik place-mats'.) The Greek camp is not so much a military encampment as an ethnic crafts bazaar. If diplomacy is war minus the shooting, Petersen's Trojan War is Glastonbury minus the mud, a cleaned-up global village. All the usual festival paraphernalia is here: the yurts, the dreadlocks, the hippy hemp clothing and, above all, the tragic addiction to beads and 'tribal' costume jewellery. At times it seems that Petersen's lovingly CGId thousand ships – count 'em – have come to Troy, not for glory or conquest, but to corner the international imitation-jade market. Achilles, Agamemnon, Priam's boys – none of them can get enough beads into their outfits, their armour, or their hair.

At the same time, this is 'ethnic' as comfortably conceived by rich Beverly Hills boys – i.e. without any of that scarily different *actual* ethnicity. The film's sharper reviewers pointed out that *Troy* is, despite its pretensions ('from an idea by Homer'), not so much a film of the *Iliad* as of the Epic Cycle: thematically threadbare, ploddingly linear. It's true that Petersen's film seems to owe more to the artless 'and then this happened' storytelling of (mostly lost) epics like the *Cypria* and *Aethiopis* than to Homer's own tightly plotted and structurally quite adventurous *Iliad*. But what opportunities have been missed, given the sheer breadth of storytelling the Cycle encompassed: from Penthesilea and her Amazons to Memnon, Troy's great ally, warrior king of the Ethiopians. A truly diverse epic could have found room for these and more. (After all, everything else is in there.) Xena might be visually a shoo-in for a *Troy* cameo but, on this evidence, she'd have rapidly become very bored there. Her own franchise is, unsurprisingly, happily multi-ethnic.

Troy, then, struggled from the start to close down meaning into comfortably familiar shapes via marketing strategies, characterisation and mise-en-scène (however badly that last one worked out in practice). Perhaps commercial considerations made this attempt a necessary one; but the film that resulted from it still smacks of missed opportunity, and not just for classicists and other pedants. At the same time, its underwhelming commercial performance underscores the issues we have explored in the present chapter. By situating its ancient-world storyline outside the (fitfully) saleable framework of stock Roman narratives, *Troy* found itself without a viable template for its ostentatiously confused take on heroic masculinity. Instead, and with alternative media texts like *300* fanning the flames, critics and audiences slotted *Troy* straight into the same old half-contemptuous conversations about Greece and the Greeks, with what by now should be very predictable consequences. Reviewers queued up to ridicule – or semi-mockingly celebrate – its deliciously oblivious camp subtexts. Boys, boys, boys:

> Brad is so hunky that I expected the Trojan troops to surrender immediately, and hand over not only Helen but their phone numbers scrawled on matchbooks … This is a movie about why there are so many gay guys named Troy … And maybe there were other ancient cities called David and Scott. Brad is … like a bipolar florist called in at the last minute to save the royal wedding reception.

Whether any of this directly reflects the content of the film itself is, I suggest, beside the point. The cumulative and fraught post-Victorian ideological baggage of 'Greece' is such that there can *be* no 'film itself'. The circumstances *Troy* inherited ruled out any possibility of it standing alone as a safely bounded artistic work, answering only to itself or to its creator, magnificently apart and immune from the diverse appetites and fixed preconceptions of contemporary popular culture. Instead it found itself walled in by decades, if not centuries, of assigned values and accreted meanings – trapped in the Maze of the Minotaur with Theocritus, Dan Vadis and John Addington Symonds. In turning its back on the diversity, reflexivity and sheer fun of contemporary receptions within participatory popular culture, *Troy* ignored a potential Ariadne's thread that might have led it out of the labyrinth into new cinematic territory.

Where could Greek heroism, and the *peplum*, go from here? In the final chapter we will consider Oliver Stone's mammoth *Alexander*, fondly but dismissively dubbed 'Olly's Folly' by a bemused media. *Troy* founders on half-measures in its approach to mise-en-scène and sources; *Alexander* set out to avoid its mistakes, with a surprising degree of success. So what *did* go wrong? Again, the story will take us back to the fifties and beyond – and, again, the answers will shed surprising light on what 'Greece' can be made to mean in a new millennium.

3

WARS OF THE SUCCESSORS

Greece's mythic misadventures have left its legendary leading man trapped in a Herculean double bind; do its historical heroics fare any better? As we saw in ch.1, cinema needs to keep the audience-unfriendly big Ideas of Greek history – politics, art, philosophy – out of the frame. That ought to leave plenty of classic action-adventure narratives for the multiplexes, cherry-picked from a centuries-long history at least as violent as Rome's. Hollywood's canon of bankable Greek history is narrow, however; just two stories stand out. One is Thermopylae, the Greek Alamo. As an interpretative staging point in its context-driven approach to Petersen's *Troy*, ch.2 showed how receptions of Thermopylae in modern popular culture initially set up this last stand of muscular heroism (no high-brow politics or philosophy here) for failure and, indeed, bathos, via ironised nostalgia and a wilfully applied camp aesthetic – to say nothing of the creeping Romanisation which by now seems par for the course if not positively inescapable. It is entertainingly ironic that the Spartans, ultra-conservative and purity-fixated Hellenic separatists, blur so quickly into Roman bogeyman Spartacus and immediately bog down in borrowed commie / queer kitsch.

Cinema's other A-List Hellenic narrative, of course, is Alexander the Great, a ready-made, larger-than-life crowd-pleaser with truly global appeal – from Hollywood to Bollywood and beyond.

(Alexander even gets his own Japanese *manga* series.) Alexander is not only filmable; he ought to be bankable. But things are never that simple where receptions of Greece are concerned. Ch.1 introduced a number of easily available case studies-*cum*-cautionary tales of well-intentioned, capable auteurs finding that Greece was more of a mouthful than they had bargained for. This chapter begins by adding to their number, showing how Robert Rossen's intelligent and conscientious *Alexander the Great* (1956) fell apart at the seams. It is in many ways tempting – and legitimate, and indeed productive – to read Oliver Stone's *Alexander* (2004) as a 'remake' of Rossen's film. However, my account of *Troy* makes it clear that we can't leave it at that. Instead, my account of *Alexander* follows ch.2 in insisting on broader, contemporary contexts in participatory popular culture.

There are important differences of emphasis. The contextualisation of *Troy* in ch.2 began by casting backwards to the sixties *pepla* and beyond to put the problems of Greek muscle in perspective. (Of course, these are problems which necessarily confront *Alexander* too; as we'll see, cheap-and-cheerful sixties receptions continue to inflect Alexander's ongoing narrative in surprising ways.) I then engaged with a fairly limited range of contemporary (sub-)cultural products to show how these problems continue to hamstring the Greek heroics of popular culture. This approach reflected, among other factors, *Troy*'s status as self-conscious, arty one-off, a status I was concerned to demystify: there turned out to be, really, no such thing as 'the film itself'. Stone's *Alexander*, on the other hand, offers rich pickings for a context-driven cultural studies approach: it never pretended to stand in isolation. Instead, right from the start, *Alexander* found itself caught up in a race for success against a slew of rival projects. Alexander himself has been dead for nearly two and a half millennia, but he refuses to stay buried; in the mid- to late 1990s he was hardly ever out of the media gossip columns and often in the news headlines. Critics, fans and would-be rivals endlessly and sometimes viciously thrashed out fiercely competing versions of what Alexander the Great meant. In this ideologically fraught war of words, the sign of 'Alexander' was refashioned as a controversial case study in Greek identity. Was it essentially cultural, ethnic or geographic – or was it *all* up for grabs? Battle lines were drawn up, and Alexander became a manifesto and rallying-cry. Descriptive and prescriptive versions of Alexander faced off against each other, only to find themselves merging: university textbooks blurred into political tracts. (Perhaps it had always already been that way; but that's another, much larger story.) Was Alexander really 'Greek', and if so, *how* Greek? Who were the 'Greeks', anyway? For a few wonderful, insane years, the warring *Alexanders* slogged it out, Successor-style, for control of his legacy and thus of his meaning – and told us things we never knew about receptions of classical antiquity. The Western world that Alexander helped create was again at war for possession of his long-vanished bones. We might even be encouraged by this to go further and experiment with a kind of reception-studies-in-reverse. Star image and PR were, after all, key to the Successor generals' race for ancient market share in the aftermath of Alexander's death.

Oliver Stone's *Alexander* (2004) was, of course, the eventual winner of the modern race. Like Petersen's *Troy*, this impeccably intentioned if flawed film now feeds a thriving critical mini-industry. Once again I see more profit in sounding out the film's imaginative hinterland than in joining the queue to pick holes in the blockbuster itself, fun though that undeniably is. My story begins, naturally enough, with the film of which Stone's is a virtual remake, Robert Rossen's *Alexander the Great* (1956); but it also enlists Baz Luhrmann's perennially just-round-the-corner *Alexander*, a film that will in all likelihood never be made, alongside a gamut of more or less 'forthcoming' Alexander projects, ranging from the sublime to the ridiculous. Realistically, these films were never going to make it to the screen (or not *all* of them); but they deserve serious consideration as the touchstones of the 1990s / 2000s Alexander debate. Stone's *Alexander* emerges as merely one chapter in a much larger story – and not the final chapter at that: the story is still going strong. My account also entails reference to *Cleopatra* (1963), where a former Alexander (Burton, playing Antony) mourns drunkenly on the death of his earlier promise; he might as well be weeping for Alexander's prospects in the 1990s and beyond, although all hope is perhaps not yet lost.

Consideration of Luhrmann's project also leads us inexorably towards a legendarily 'lost' iteration of Alexander's mythic history: the William Shatner pilot for a never-made *Alexander the Great* TV series. The show has singular and surprising virtues as a witty commentary on the Alexander myth; but the fan / critical discourse that has grown up around it (a reception of a reception?) is equally revealing, particularly in the way it has punched so far above its weight in the Alexander-wars of the 1990s and 2000s. Popular culture continues to manufacture Alexander's legend, but his story refuses to be owned or controlled, and continually gets to us where we live. Like his rival generals in the modern conspiracy-theories, desperate to stop the myth so they could get off, we're still casting around for ways to keep Alexander at a comfortable distance – whether via academic impersonality, politicised tunnel vision or self-consciously kitschy cult nostalgia.

The canonical modern version: Robert Rossen, *Alexander the Great* (1956)

It is men who endure toil and dare danger, that achieve glorious deeds, and it is a lovely thing to live with courage and to die leaving behind an everlasting renown.

(Richard Burton's voiceover to opening credits)

Starring Richard Burton, *Alexander the Great* (1956) is a thoughtful and ambitious treatment of Alexander's life, exploits and ambitions. Mirroring the subject's autocratic career, the film is relatively tightly controlled by a single creator, Robert Rossen, who wrote, directed and produced. This was in fact Rossen's characteristic modus operandi, and a productive one at that; his other pictures as writer-director-producer include *All the King's Men* (1947) and *The Hustler* (1961).

Rossen is well supported by his crew. The rousing score by Mario Nascimbene, whose previous soundtrack credits included *The Vikings* (1958) and *Barabbas* (1961), is atmospheric and effective. Spain's sweeping vistas, presented in the still-new widescreen CinemaScope format, stand in very well for Alexander's endless East. Above all, the picture is intelligently cast. Transcending a regrettable blond rinse, the youngish Burton projects an intense screen presence, fighting first for his father's attention and then to turn himself into a living legend. The supporting ensemble of talented Brits includes Barry Jones (Aristotle); Michael Hordern (Demosthenes); Harry Andrews (Darius); *Helen of Troy*'s Achilles, Stanley Baker (Attalus); and future Hammer Horror regular, Peter Cushing, as the honour-bound Greek mercenary leader Memnon. (Memnon and Demosthenes would be reunited eighteen years later in the cult Hammer picture, *Theatre of Blood* (1973).) Rossen, whose background is in theatre, extracts nuanced performances.

Right from the start, the production announces itself as a bid for the 'real' Alexander – or, at least, for a plausible simulacrum. The credits roll to stark, primitive drums and trumpets; the first image we see is a gold coin, bearing Alexander's portrait. The film's title is overlaid in an angular typeface, suggesting an unearthed inscription, including some authentic Greek letter-forms. A further and pointed assertion of the film's regard for historical truth comes with the announcement of H.R.H. Prince Peter of Greece as historical adviser.

As the credits fade, a medium-long establishing shot presents a white marble colonnade. Figures can be seen lurking there; immediately we wonder whether we will recognise the names as historical. The establishing shot's superimposed caption, in arty red lower-case, is encouragingly precise; it is also persuasively downbeat:

> It is the year 356 BC, in a troubled, exhausted, divided, bloody Greece.

Right from the start, Rossen's film transcends the inherent gaudiness of Technicolor to present a strikingly different ancient world. The early fifties Roman epics – *Quo Vadis* (1951), *The Robe* (1953), *Demetrius and the Gladiators* (1954) – were already gearing up for the ever-increasing visual overload which would characterise the toga film until its collapse in the early sixties; indeed, *The Robe* was the showpiece film that ushered in the CinemaScope revolution. Rossen borrows *The Robe*'s new super-widescreen world view but sidesteps the parades and robes of the toga spectaculars. From the start, *Alexander*'s moody lighting, close-in cinematography and muted palettes teasingly refuse to deliver the enhanced spectacle that was CinemaScope's selling point, junking *The Robe*'s jaw-dropping panoramas to emphasise the world-weary pessimism of its themes.

The colonnade is brightly sunlit, but the shadows are gathering over Greece. Two Athenian statesmen, Demosthenes (Hordern) and Aeschines (William Squire), debate the case for war against the half-barbarian aggressor, Philip of Macedon. Rossen's cinematography reacts against Hollywood norms to create a strange new ancient world; he deliberately flouts the **180° rule**, and impressionistically sketches Philip's conquests via **montage**, with Demosthenes' pro-war rhetoric as voice-over. This process of de-familiarisation is reinforced at the level of mise-en-scène. Philip is every bit the non-Greek 'barbarian' of Demosthenes' rhetoric, a shaggy, boozed-up bandit in caveman-style furs; and his cold, torch-lit Macedonia

is a far cry from the gleaming marble of Demosthenes' (and Socrates') Athens. (Stone will take cues from it.) Philip's palace is half
Greek, half Other, stocked with random salvage: crude indigenous
art, quasi-Mycenaean lions and classical statuary. I mocked this
tendency for lucky-dip set dressing in *The Colossus of Rhodes*, but
in Rossen's bandit-country Macedonia it feels right. The cultural
plunder includes a cast-off Greek thinker, Aristotle (Jones), who
sets to work moulding the young Alexander into a philosopher-
king, convinced of his superiority as a true-blue Hellene. Under
his tuition, the future king internalises 'a divine mission, to bring
Greek culture and civilisation to all the world'. Aristotle sugars the
message with sound-bites from the classics, quoting (accurately)
from Sophocles' *Antigone* as he lectures the prince and his companions on their duty to Hellenic culture:

Wonders are many; but none is more wonderful than man
himself.

Aristotle's project of global Hellenism will not pan out as intended.
Ironically, Alexander will end up starring in his very own Greek
tragedy – or Rossen's idea of Shakespeare's idea of one. From early
in the film, Burton's Alexander sees his world as a stage, to which he
stands as audience and critic as well as soliloquy-hogging protagonist. Welcomed into conquered Athens by Demosthenes and the
appeaser Aeschines, he compliments them on their performances:

Alexander: How 'humble' is your home, Aeschines?
Aeschines: Almost Macedonian: empty hall, save victories.
Alexander: Well said.
Demosthenes: And well rehearsed.
Alexander: And well acted. In Macedonia I have heard that in
all Greece there are no two better actors than Demosthenes and
Aeschines. I should like, before I leave, to witness a perform-
ance ...

Memnon and his Persian wife Barsine, both fans of Athenian culture, share a similar frame of reference, quoting the central debate of *Antigone* between Creon and Haemon as Barsine pleads with her husband to compromise with Alexander:

> For you, Memnon – I plead for you.

Memnon will later compare Alexander to 'a hungry lion, on the scent of blood' – echoing the form and content of Homer's famous extended similes. But Alexander will not remain a passive reader and audience member. As he moves east, he drifts from epic onto the stage, metamorphosing into a tragic tyrant. Later, his dear friend Cleitus will inspire the King's murderous rage by quoting the plays back at him:

> 'Shall one man claim the trophies won by thousands?' I quote from Euripides – your favourite poet.

Alexander has learned his heroic anger from Homer's Achilles, his role-model of choice (and at the top of Aristotle's reading-list); now it turns against him, as his epic turns into a tragedy. His inflexibility is shaken, not just by Cleitus' death, but by a succession of suicides, reported in stylised 'messenger speeches'. Finding Darius dead by his own hand, Alexander hears that his final words were 'some words I didn't understand well, about destiny and fate', and is handed a parting letter – Darius' moralising soliloquy refuses to die with him. Attalus (Baker) brings news of the suicide of Philip's second wife, a young bride slighted by Alexander:

> Is the tale too horrible for your ears, King? Shall I tell you, too, who placed the noose around her pretty, white young neck? But I am a religious man, and accept the will of the gods. What's man's fate is man's fate, both yours and mine.

If anything, the frame of reference is *too* literary. Rossen is a screen-writer first and foremost, a words man; he can't leave his tragic poets alone. Even at the film's downbeat and abrupt ending, as the camera pans skyward, a voice-over solemnly reminds us (again) that 'wonders are many, but none is more wonderful than man himself'. What is more, the film's literary borrowings are as hit-and-miss as its iconography. Darius' death-bed letter quotes loosely from Shel-ley's *Ozymandias*; earlier, advised of Alexander's invasion, Darius paraphrases the Dauphin in Shakespeare's *Henry V*, dictating an insulting letter which even echoes the Dauphin's gift of tennis balls:

> Wherefore we command you: withdraw and return, go back to the bosom of your mother Olympias. For you are still an impu-dent and shameless boy … I send you a whip, a ball, and a bag of gold … the ball, so that you may play with boys of your own age, and not meddle in the affairs of men.

And Burton's Alexander responds in part, playing out young Prince Hal in the run-up to Agincourt:

> For I am coming against you, having entrusted myself to the immortal gods. I shall be victorious over you.

He reassures his troops, scared by an eclipse, that 'the gods are on our side'; before the battle, he even indulges in a late-night soliloquy to a 'god of fear' who seems a very close match for Henry's 'God of battles'. Of course, Shakespeare has already given Rossen a seem-ingly perfect excuse for all this playing around – Harry and his gang at Harfleur are billed as 'like so many Alexanders' – but the director can't let the simile lie. The casting compounds the problem. With the exception of Stanley Baker, British cinema's hard man of the moment, the main players are all theatre veterans: Rossen's kind of people, competing for the best (and longest) lines. And details of casting conspire to undercut the self-important rhetoric. Launching the invasion of Persia, Alexander reminds his generals (and us) of Aristotle's reading list – again – by a soliloquy on the figure of Achilles, Homer's archetypal Greek invader of the East:

> At Troy, Achilles found his Hector, and killed him. Who will be my Hector?

Alexander's Hector will of course be Darius, played by Harry Andrews – fresh from *Helen of Troy* (1956), where he played Hector. Is this an in-joke, or the accidental outcome of the director's jobs-for-the-boys approach to casting? Either way, the result, self-consciously and at length, is a self-regardingly 'clever' film that prefers to tell (and ideally to lecture) than to show: a movie that fails to move.

It is also an iconographic mess. Rossen scores points with the classicists by name-checking all the right historical characters and incidents (or more than Stone will) – Hephaestion, Memnon, the cutting of the Gordian Knot, the burning of Persepolis and Miletus. But the detail is often patchiest when the film is trying hardest for 'authenticity'. The title sequence sets the pattern: 'ALEXANDER THE GREAT' has the hard angularity of a Greek inscription, but it achieves its look by grabbing Greek letter-forms that don't fit. The Greek capital 'E' (*epsilon*) looks just like ours, but that doesn't look *Greek* enough – so the film-makers substitute *sigmas*, Σ. The result looks great, even if it does read 'ALSXANDER THS GRSAT'. (The 2002 romantic comedy *My Big Fat Greek Wedding* – or rather, *Grssk Wedding* – ran into the same titling difficulty, although this was perhaps the least of its problems.)

In a sense, this is the perennial problem of movies set in ancient Greece: *Alexander* can't simultaneously look *and* be right. (Its costuming, for instance, runs into all the usual difficulties.) But Rossen's attention to the details of Alexander's story makes the visual glitches stand out, and some of them are very curious. The

Persian chariots have the scythe-bladed wheels of *Ben-Hur* (the 1925 silent version; the Charlton Heston remake was four years away). Alexander orders that Darius' faithless bodyguards are to be impaled – but in the next shot we see them crucified. (Directorial squeamishness, or just the usual problem – that Roman iconographies are always wandering into the edge of the shot?) Alexander and his generals plot their strategy on a vellum map, complete with place-names – Latin ones (the Black Sea, for instance, is labelled *Pontus Euxinus*). Alexander's own armour is a Caesarean cast-off, copied from the famous Prima Porta statue of the emperor Augustus. Greece's Prince Peter has done little to earn his cheque.

If anything, Rossen's narrative seriousness makes the discrepancies more glaring; his denial of spectacle, at first so intriguing, begins to wear thin. The battle sequences are lacklustre, wasting a large cast of extras. Alexander's Indian conquests are glossed over in montage, again to a voice-over of accusatory Athenian rhetoric. Many sets are perfunctory, more akin to theatrical 'flats' than to fully realised locations. Rossen's establishing shot of the Athenian colonnade is a case in point: the detailing of the columns is fine, but what is the colonnade *for*? It can't keep the sun off, the usual reason for building one, as there is no roof. It doesn't resemble any kind of real building, ancient or modern (although it bears a passing resemblance to the pre-ruined Greece of Corman's *Atlas*). It's a symbol for 'Greek building', with the pared-down simplicity that makes for good theatre design; but this aesthetic transfers badly to film sets.

The visual field of Rossen's *Alexander* is additionally impoverished by bowdlerisation. Rossen labours to purge his mise-en-scène of any reference to nudity, particularly male. Even canonical art is regarded as unsafe: in Philip's palace at Pella, Myron's classic 'discus-thrower' is turned to face the wall. At the gymnasium, Alexander and his companions exercise wearing trunks, rather than naked as the

Greeks famously did; they are inspired in their training by statues of victorious athletes, heroically nude – but with fig-leaves to cover their modesty. The precedents Rossen has in mind are presumably Victorian; but his mise-en-scène more immediately, if inadvertently, recalls the ersatz-classical sculptural schemes of Mussolini's Fascist sports complexes. Many of the muscular and ponderously allegorical athlete figures with which Rome's Foro Italico in particular is crammed were fig-leaved – or even put in shorts – to appease contemporary sensibilities (Fig. 9). Even Pella's *herms* (good-luck fertility images) lose their tackle – and with it, their meaning. Dressing down Demosthenes and Aeschines in Athens, Alexander pointedly contrasts the Athenians of his day to the 'wonderful physiques' of the statues with which they fill their Acropolis; but the statues he praises have been mutilated by the prudery of Rossen's production. We might prefer to be Aeschines, with his pot belly: rather that than a hard-bodied eunuch.

The source of the film's extraordinary anxiety about the male body beautiful has to be Hephaestion, Alexander's close male companion. Rossen's enthusiasm for historical name-checking mandates his inclusion; but what is the film to do with him? Male same-sex attraction was – and remains – Hollywood's greatest taboo; and Rossen's scripting and casting of Hephaestion speak volumes. Is he a general, a friend, or something more? The ancient sources leave the issue hanging, leaving plenty of room for speculation by later historians and other interested parties: Rossen, however, ducks the question entirely. Like the Hylas of Hercules' twentieth-century receptions, his Hephaestion is a nonentity, a gaping absence in the narration. His redundancy is underlined by brutally tactical casting: shut out by a tight ensemble of strong and experienced British players, Italian third-stringer Ricardo Valle is outclassed from the start and leaves no impression on the audience – just the effect that was needed.

9. Covering up at Rome's Foro Italico: *Alexander the Great* (1955) is one of many *pepla* to reflect longstanding anxieties about the sexual politics of Greek athletic nudity.

The result of this too-insistent denial, of course, is a film with strong camp potential; but also a film that seems to have lost its nerve – and its sense of fun – at a very early stage. There is still pleasure, even for purists, in the literate script; and Richard Burton's performance remains watchable, a relative high-water mark in his on-and-off love affair with Hollywood's ancient world. Years later, amid the snowballing chaos of *Cleopatra* (1963), we can watch as a paunchy, visibly unwell Burton (playing Marc Antony) drunkenly mourns the premature death of his early promise as a film actor. Slouched against the now legendarily lost tomb of his brooding and intense young Alexander, a famous drunk (played by a famous drunk) weeping for a famous drunk (ditto), he rants against Cleo, Liz, and stardom's roads not taken:

> Time for what? For Marc Antony to appear in shining armour, swords flashing in both hands? Pfff, Agrippa! Pfff, Octavian! 'Stand back, rejoice, Marc Antony will save the day!'.

If it hadn't been for Burton's youthful flirtation with corrupting 'Greek' ways, his Antony could have been a Roman contender. By the time of *Cleopatra*, though, his intrusively reported alcoholism had turned the actor into a natural Antony – and, belatedly, into a model 'late' Alexander. His boozy, stagnant pessimism bleeds through into Stone's *Alexander*, infected as it is with Rossen's leaden pacing and fatal deference to the dead hand of Alexander scholarship.

We can note in passing that by implicitly following in Rossen's tracks – but then backing off – Stone's *Alexander* sells itself short; but Rossen is only a small part of this story. We shall see that *Alexander*'s frustrating inability to add up to the sum of its parts reflects its failure to articulate a distinctive response to a range of largely conservative contemporary discourses of Alexander. (Actually, *Alexander* is almost entirely reactive; even its director's rhetoric of heroic auteurist individuality marks him as one of the herd.) Bizarrely, *Alexander* ends up closing down its available options in order to distance itself from films that never actually got made, most particularly Luhrmann's. That film, one which might have moved the modern Alexander on (or rather given us a *post*-modern Alexander), presently languishes in Development Hell; Stone's, meanwhile, lost its way in a long, Babylon-bound retreat from pressure groups and fan bases. One particularly telling example of this is the surprising negative influence exercised by ironic-nostalgic 1990s receptions of a 1960s Alexander, of whom most classicists and film buffs (and even Alexander *aficionados*) had previously been unaware. Fatally, this was an Alexander who knew how to have *fun*; an Alexander who was instantly, if only semi-seriously, recuperated as a Luhrmann prototype. In this way, and largely because of – of all things – *Star Trek* **fandom**, an obscure, no-budget sixties reception became a stalking horse for Stone's mammoth project.

The 'lost' Alexander who won't go away: the 1964 television pilot

The pilot episode for a series that was never made, and legendarily unobtainable, the William Shatner *Alexander the Great* is referred to today in hushed tones, as befits an early work of the man who would be Kirk. It's next to impossible to speak of the Shatner *Alexander* as if *Star Trek* had never happened – to say nothing of *T. J. Hooker*, *Airplane: II* and the infamous Beatles cover versions. The appearance of Adam West (soon to be TV's Batman) as the Greek general Cleander only adds fuel to the fire. Nor is it clear that we *should* try to keep Shatner's subsequent star image out of the picture. Try as we might, we can't turn back time and make it 1968 again, the year in which the pilot was eventually broadcast; by then, in any case, *Star Trek's* five-year mission was well under way, and Shatner was a star.

In this sense, *Alexander the Great* never really *had* an 'original' audience. In any case, the added pleasure here for a Trek-aware audience is undeniable. The pilot is rarely mentioned in published discussions of Greek movies; but it casts a long shadow within film and television fandom, where it has become progressively mythologised by Shatner *aficionados* and detractors (usually the same people) as a lost icon of heroic bad taste. Fan discourse explicitly interprets the show in the light of the performers' subsequent careers, pitching it at a contemporary audience acclimatised to Shatner's eventual, graceful slide into arch self-parody:

> But nowadays, it's a wet dream come true for TV icon watchers ... true High Camp indeed ... I'll bet even Adam West was embarrassed.
> I almost recommend this just for the camp factor!

One prolific **blogger** wrote, in connection with Oliver Stone's then-forthcoming *Alexander*:

> Hey, here's a great idea: Stone should find a role for Shatner in the new movie. During breaks between filming, Shatner could even entertain the '60s-fixated Stone with renditions of a Shatner classic: 'Lucy in the Sky with Diamonds'.

Crucial to the totemic status of the pilot in the narratives of fans and critics (again, in the internet age, the distinction is hard to maintain) is its legendary status as a 'lost' one-off. The Shatner pilot is in fact one of two famously missing and / or unobtainable versions which helped define the nineties debate: *Sikander*, a 1940s Indian musical version, was also at times namedropped as an end-stop for Luhrmann's project. (It's worthy of note that other and perhaps equally interesting Alexanders were potentially available to inform the nineties debate, notably the 1961 BBC remake of Terence Rattigan's *Adventure Story*, starring Sean Connery; but that Connery's appropriation-resistant star image kept *Adventure Story* out of 1990s Alexander-discourse.) While Shatner's *Alexander* remains tantalisingly unseen, the kitsch appeal of the star's flabby later career can be projected backwards onto this early venture, playing up its perceived camp aspects. It's startling, then, to find that the pilot enjoyed a successful limited theatrical release in Europe; still more so to discover that (unlike *Sikander*) it can be quickly and easily acquired in a choice of VHS and DVD formats via Internet auction sites such as Ebay. Nor do fans seem to be falling over themselves to take advantage of this ready availability; many seem to prefer a 'lost' legend. (Adam West's signed and personally annotated copy of the script recently changed hands on the Sotheby's auction website for a mere $144 including premiums, well under half the anticipated price – a steal.)

Issues of fan discourse aside, the pilot deserves much more attention than it has tended to receive. Inevitably, the picture quality is poor; many generations of tape duplication stand between currently available copies and the original broadcast. Yet the show remains compelling. As actual television rather than internet urban legend, the *Alexander* pilot shatters all preconceptions. The production is cheap, but looks good: the crucial battle scenes are impressively handled. The script is highly literate and contains many pleasurable surprises for Alexander fans. And Shatner himself is a revelation. He is still young, lean and ambitious; the *Alexander* pilot antedates his run on *Star Trek* by a year. His Shakespearean background is evident here as never in his lazier later work, both in the physical vigour of his performance and in the moral complexity he brings to the role. His interpretation of *Alexander* bears comparison to his dark and driven performance as the racist demagogue Adam Cramer in Roger Corman's viscerally compelling *The Intruder* (1961). Like Cramer, Shatner's Alexander is charismatic but rootless, a drifter. An energetic and forceful presence throughout, he mounts horses at a leap, duels with panache (his stage training coming to the fore) and both charms and dominates his assembled generals. But he is also secretive and emotional, a compulsive serial risk-taker, a man who is happy to pretend to be a god; a figure of hinted menace and, potentially, a madman.

Even in this first episode, these tensions within Alexander are tearing his army apart. His most loyal generals already question his rationality; two of them conspire to betray him – but reluctantly, compelled to plot against the king they love by their greater love for their homeland. They are convinced that Alexander's obsessive insistence on pre-emptive aggression will destroy Greece. Watching the *Alexander* pilot for the first time in March 2003, with the second Gulf War already bogging down, I found it hard to condemn the generals; their fears seemed well grounded.

Tensions within the group run high, and everyone is putting on some kind of act – Alexander above all. Even Alexander's most reliable adherent, the cautious Antigonus (Orson Welles regular Joseph Cotten), seems more concerned to make a spectacle of his loyalty than to fulfil his responsibilities as a father-figure to the impetuous young king. The conspirators attempt to recruit him; although he should keep silent and warn Alexander, he cannot resist the opportunity to declaim dramatically against them, and is quickly done away with. (The moment has added shock value for viewers in the know about events after Alexander's death; as the future founder of a Hellenistic dynasty, Antigonus surely *can't* die yet.) The ringleader Karonos (John Cassavetes), saturnine and intense, is Alexander's dynamic right-hand man: *Henry V*-like, Alexander takes his betrayal as a personal rejection by the man who knew 'the very bottom of my soul'. Distraught, he seeks Karonos out during the climactic battle with the effete Persian general Memnon (comedy actor Cliff Osmond). The duel is simultaneously a mutual seduction and, despite the large-scale excitement of the surrounding mêlée, the mood is curiously intimate. Is the fictional 'Karonos' part Hephaistion? The shots are set up to make the pair seem suddenly and paradoxically alone in the crowd; and lingering close-ups show them looking intently (longingly?) into each other's eyes:

> Alexander: Karonos, I've been looking a long while for you.
> Karonos: And I, you.

The two men tussle energetically but almost clumsily; we have seen both of them fight much better. Alexander stabs Karonos / Hephaistion, sliding his blade in deep; there is time for another long, soul-searching exchange of glances before the traitor falls, rolling down the hillside, the skirt of his tunic bunched up around his waist. After the battle, the camera pans slowly across a silent battlefield strewn with corpses. Left momentarily alone, a mounted Alexander looks back over his shoulder in melancholy regret at Karonos' death. Then, with studied cynicism, and making sure we get his best side, he re-arranges his features into the mask of the Man of Destiny. Even without an audience (or with only us as his audience), the arch-narcissist cannot help putting on an act. A skilled manipulator, he knows exactly how to play upon the fears and doubts of his generals, including their doubts as to his sanity – doubts which we, the audience at home, have by now come to share and upon which Alexander himself is careful to offer no comment. Is there a real personality behind the obsessively maintained façade, beneath the trademark, carefully tousled mop of blond curls – or is he nothing but surface? If this Alexander is a psychopath – and Shatner's disquieting performance conveys that possibility very ably – then he is a fascinatingly self-aware one. As the credits roll, the cautious survivors, cowed by their leader's exemplary violence, follow him on horseback into the East; their swords held pointlessly, phallically erect in slavish imitation of their unbalanced generalissimo.

The persistent characterisation of the *Alexander* pilot as more or less irretrievably 'lost' has concealed the show's darker, more thoughtful aspects. (My own reading of the show – and of Shatner's complicated, charismatic, potentially monstrous Alexander – reacts against this routine trivialisation and is consciously and obviously partial.) In the absence of the show itself, fandom's ongoing dialogue about it has taken on a life of its own. Tarred with the brush of later Shatner – and, indeed, of Adam West's Batman – the pilot has been caricatured as an unintentional classic of sixties kitsch. The fans can hardly be blamed; Shatner's subsequent descent into knowingly camp self-parody (with *Boston Legal* its logical end-point … for now) makes the process of 'reading back' well-nigh irresistible. The show's status as 'lost', however spurious, makes possible some very enjoyable retrospective fantasies – essentially a variant on the slash fiction generated by the evolving subcultures of *Star Trek* fandom. (If only a supporting role had gone to Leonard Nimoy …)

The misrepresentation of the pilot as 'lost' is not only understandable; it can be read productively. The ascendancy of self-interested myth-making over a more prosaic actual history is very like what has happened to the figure of Alexander himself over time – ever since his death, in fact, as his surviving generals fell out over his legacy, tweaked their Alexander-clone coin portraits and carved out the Successor States. There is even good evidence to suggest that Alexander himself was a skilled if erratic manipulator of the Alexander myth during his own lifetime. He was an obsessive controller of his own visual image – the coin-portraits imitated by his generals had already morphed Alexander into Apollo and Zeus Ammon; and also a calculating patron of flattering campaign journals and propaganda-laden epic poems (although later writers criticise his simplistic literary judgement). The warlords who bickered over the remnants of Alexander's empire continued and built upon a game of myth-making that had already acquired an unstoppable momentum.

An important early move in this game of spin and spectacle, claim and counter-claim, was the ownership of Alexander's physical remains. One general, Ptolemy, soon to restyle himself 'Ptolemy the First' and 'the Saviour', hijacked the body *en route* to Macedonia and installed it in a splendid tomb in his new (and likewise hijacked) capital of Alexandria in Egypt. Modern popular awareness of this tomb begins with *Cleopatra* (1963) and Burton's self-referentially soused moping; its uncertain whereabouts continue to furnish good copy. In classical antiquity, the tomb was a magnet for publicity-aware despots with ambitions to make like Alexander and rule the world – Caesar, Octavian, Germanicus. But it was later to become shrouded in mystery. Today, much of ancient Alexandria is gone for good, and scholars speculate endlessly over the body's final resting place – yet more Alexander myth-making. The tomb's status as 'lost' – just like that of the Shatner *Alexander* pilot – adds to its glamour; the missing body is fuel for the documentaries and conspiracy theories of the Alexander industry, wherever scholarship (the more partisan, the better) intersects with popular culture. The less is known, the richer the pickings for the modern myth-makers.

Even trivialised as mindless kitsch, then, the 1964 pilot can help us towards a more nuanced understanding of the rag-bag of stories we call 'Alexander' – just as the sixties muscleman *pepla* teased out an authentic (fake) 'Hercules'. Taken seriously as an intelligent response to Alexander's own myth-making, it offers further thought-provoking narrative twists. I have already touched on the Shakespearean inflections of Shatner's performance and how productive they are for the show. His stage background, reflected in a sympathetic script, enables him to sketch out a complex, contradictory, ironic and archly 'post-Rossen' Alexander who rewards repeated viewing. (Clearly, too, a hint of the Bard must have been calculated to help establish the respectability and prestige of this relatively low-budget TV venture, with its still near-unknown leading man.) In particular, *Alexander*'s evocation and subsequent 'rewriting' of Julius Caesar is a resonant narrative gambit, with pointed (and multiple) relevance to the ongoing mythic construction of Alexander from antiquity onwards. Plutarch paired the two conquerors up for a bravura compare-and-contrast in his cross-cultural parallel biographies, the *Lives* – an important source for Shakespeare's Caesar, too. In antiquity, the media-friendly soldier king of Macedon was quickly turned by historians and poets into an indispensable but dangerous template for elite Romans who fancied themselves in the role of larger-than-life world ruler. Caesar's visit to his tomb was just the first of a series of easily misinterpreted photo-opportunities; Antony's was surely another. Later would-be emperors, Napoleon included, added their own layers of complication. So, too, did a succession of post-Shakespearean media representations; Shatner's brooding, tight-wound performance is among other things an inspired steal from Brando's Antony in MGM's 1953 *Julius Caesar*.

For contemporary culture, then, 'Alexander' is not a single historical person; he's an accretion of narrative strata laid down by successive versions of the story, some of them acted out by the most unlikely of candidates. Compared to Napoleon, Shatner is a natural for the part; and the 1964 pilot remains the only modern version that not only acknowledges but gets its teeth into the multiplicity, the open-endedness (inherent in the TV-serial format) and the sheer messiness of the Alexander myth. It stands the test of time and emerges as a self-aware and adroit commentary on a game of spin and counter-spin which, in the early years of the third millennium, is as fraught and relevant as it ever was. Ironically, this hour-long slice of disposable and seemingly unsuccessful genre TV – like Alexander, it completely failed to establish an ongoing 'succession' via syndication – is a contender for the twentieth century's most significant version of the Alexander story.

In many ways, too, it has set up the conditions for future retellings in film – in particular, via the involvement of Adam West as the (made-up) general Cleander. Again, star image, in this case the baggage of West's later career, leads the fans of High Camp to read more back into the role than the script and production can support. The cast list generates the verdicts independently of the show's content. In the pilot, Cleander is a bit part and the performances establish no chemistry between Shatner and West. In an interview by fan author Dan Epstein for a *Star Trek* appreciation website, Shatner had difficulty recalling West's involvement in the show:

> *Epstein*: I just read about an Alexander the Great pilot you did for television with Adam West.
> *Shatner*: Was Adam West in it?
> *Epstein*: Yes.
> *Shatner*: [very thoughtfully] Huh.

To add to our frustration, West himself is hard to recognise; but, of course, we're not used to seeing him from the nose up. He achieved iconic status as hero of the *Batman* TV series (1965–1968), a contemporary of the original *Star Trek* (1966–1968). With its comic-style action balloons ('Sock!', 'Pow!'), bright nursery colours and self-consciously silly dialogue, the show quickly became a byword for lovable kitsch – and a classic of camp, thanks to the tender and playful relationship it established between cohabiting bachelors Batman and Robin.

Fans of genre TV have long enjoyed the show's queer subtexts (if they can be called subtexts at all; they are perhaps too obvious). The discovery that our beloved Batman had previously played a skirt-wearing Boy Wonder to Shatner's Caped Crusader – *eromenos*, as it were, to Alexander's **erastes** – was an exquisite instance of role-reversal, really the icing on the cake. Understandably, fan appreciations of the 'lost' *Alexander* pilot find it hard to resist inter-preting Cleander as a closeted Hephaestion.

This revisionist or 'slash' reading has little or nothing to do with the actual content of the show itself – again, of course, a phrase crying out for irony quotes. (My tendentious interpreta-tion of Karonos as a veiled Hephaestion could be dismissed as a similar exercise in wishful thinking.) All the same, a queered Cleander opens up Alexander's prospects on-screen, paving the way for future gay / bisexual versions – particularly the Alexander of Baz Luhrmann's ever-forthcoming *Alexander* project. Versions of the script leaked online suggested that the hero's bisexuality would be handled with sympathetic neutrality. The ensuing internet rumour-mill also saw a conservative backlash, with a minority of modern Greeks regrettably to the fore as the self-appointed guardians of Alexander's memory. This unedifying campaign to straighten out Alexander combined crude homophobic slurs with spurious appeals to 'historical accuracy' (*sic*), attempting to blur any distinction between 'sexual perversion' and 'perversion of history'. Again, star image was read as either endorsing or threatening another wishful 'slash' characterisation: Alexander as pure-blood Hellene and family man (the emphases in these excerpts are mine):

> Alexander was not Gay, and Hephaestion was Alexander's dearest friend and confidant … some writers misinterpreted the meaning of this and ended up *perverting history* … Unfor-tunately, Baz and Oliver have chosen the *perverted version* of history.

> There is no conclusive evidence that Alexander was bisexual! It is all hearsay and interpretation by historians, from notations and stories through the ages. A man is *innocent until proven guilty* beyond a reasonable doubt in law!

What idiot would cast such a *pretty boy* debutant of an actor like
Leonardo DiCaprio as one of the greatest military leaders of all
time ... he must not know much about *the real life of Alexander*
at all.

Of course, 'the basic truth' about Alexander is forever inaccessible
to us, regardless of our views on the validity of historical methods
and the availability of historical facts. Postmodernists point out
that the past just isn't there any more; but even fairly conventional
historians would concur that Alexander is, by now, more spin than
substance. Documenting 'the real life of Alexander' isn't just an
uphill struggle; it's arguably a fool's errand – much less fun than
following the myths as they take on a life of their own. But other
myths are at stake here: myths of nationhood and of masculinity.
Alexander continues to count, vitally, in the ongoing manufacture
of these foundational stories; and the Shatner *Alexander* remained
good to think with as the squabble over Alexander's body and legacy
began to heat up once again.

A final and oblique aspect of star image qualifies Shatner as
our most thought-provoking (post-) modern Alexander to date.
In Epstein's interview with Shatner, the discussion on Alexander
segues into a new line of questioning: the star, like the king, has
become a living god. Unlike Alexander, Shatner has the grace to be
bemused by this transition:

> *Epstein*: I was reading about the First Church of Shatnerology.
> *Shatner*: What?
> *Epstein*: Someone established a church with your name in it.
> *Shatner*: Oh, my gosh. That's news to me.

No such modesty was apparent in the ambitions of the latest round
of Successors – or certainly not by the time the studio publicists
were through with them.

'Like so many Alexanders': Wars of the Successors

Who would emerge as Alexander's new heir? As late as 2003 his legacy was still hotly contested; earlier, the New York Times had characterised the race as a *Ben-Hur*-style 'multi-chariot pile-up'. As the dust began to settle, Luhrmann and Stone emerged in the forefront of the battle. Gossipy consensus favoured Baz as the front runner until very late in the day – really, until Stone started filming and he didn't. At the same time, several previously bullish projects were now clearly non-starters, including the potential 'best' *Alexander* (the McQuarrie / Scorsese project); and the rest would have to take their chances against the big two. Claims of casting decisions, or of directors shooting background footage of scenic Himalayan backdrops, went back and forward as spoiling gambits on all sides; some of these projects still list as 'in pre-production' even now, and may linger there for years more before quietly expiring. (Readers keen to track these projects to the bitter end will find some relevant web resources listed in Further Reading.)

That said, there remains a remote chance that Lurhmann's *Alexander* will eventually see the light of day. And the brouhaha that surrounds the rival Alexanders in their embryonic state is itself culturally revealing. What is Alexander, then or now, if not hype? Any attempt to succeed him – then (the Successor generals) or now (the studios and stars) – becomes an exercise in spin and self-promotion. This was a war of PR coups and well-publicised shifts of allegiance. The competitors to stay in the fight longest were, noticeably, those with the busiest publicity machines; if they kept telling us they were winning, it would surely turn out to be true. Stone was well cast as Ptolemy and Lurhmann made a fine rival dynast; Seleucus, perhaps. For now, however, I leave Stone's victorious *Alexander* out of the picture. One good reason to begin with these ultimately unsuccessful rival projects is that they are a large part of the context against which Stone's film took shape. At different times, each of the three projects with which I engage was regarded as the front-runner in the race; and many of *Alexander*'s concerns only make sense as moves in a shared game of media spin and damage-control. The casting coups and plot twists of its three main rivals underline the sheer contingency and plasticity of the film in development. This is a watered-down form of my provocative opening suggestion that there is no 'film itself' here. But we can also use these failed projects to pursue a stronger version of this contention, having to do with issues of cultural ownership, and with a focus quite distinct from media spin and Hollywood egos. The squabbles of critics, fan bases and special-interest groups, interminably debating the merits and flaws of films that would in the end be little more than pipe-dreams, were more revealing and more provocative of thought 'about Alexander' than the film that eventually reached our screens.

My focus here is on three projects with serious intentions and prospects in the mid- to late-1990s: the Lurhmann, Scorsese and Gibson *Alexanders*. I cover each concisely; if their chameleon-like changes appear bewildering, bear in mind that it could easily be worse. There were several other *Alexander* projects out there during this period, each of which adds its own ripples to the pool, but which I pass over here for reasons of space and clarity. Intrigued readers will not have to dig hard to find an art-house Alexander (by the director of *Like Water for Chocolate*); a kickboxing Alexander (directed by *Conan*'s John Milius! starring the Muscles from Brussels, Jean-Claude Van Damme!); even an angst-laden teen Alexander (the cheap-and-cheerful *Alexander the Great from Macedonia*, a kind of 'Pella 90210'). Nevertheless, I end the section with a fourth seemingly minor film project, an expatriate-Greek patriotic effort. This fourth film never stood a particularly good chance of being made but, like the Shatner *Alexander*, it ended up punching far above its weight in contemporary Alexander-discourse.

The once and future *Alexander*: Ridley Scott / Baz Luhrmann / Dino De Laurentiis

Baz Luhrmann, a long-time Alexander fan, signed on to direct this Dino De Laurentiis production in July 2002. Previously, De Laurentiis had attempted to secure *Gladiator* director Ridley Scott. Scott fed the gossip industry via interviews where he announced his 'plans' to direct De Laurentiis' *Alexander*, claiming the film had a head start on its rivals and was already in production; however, he subsequently moved on to other projects. Scott never settled on a likely leading man, although the ubiquitous Anthony Hopkins was announced in an unspecified supporting role. In retrospect, it's irresistibly tempting to read Scott's recent crusader epic *Kingdom of Heaven* (2005) as the *Alexander* he never made. In Orlando Bloom's improbably pretty blacksmith-turned-Defender of Jerusalem, Scott delivers a rehashed 'progressive' Alexander, driven to fight by a vision of peace, understanding and cultural fusion between East and West. This early twentieth century spin on Alexander, most famously linked to the Cambridge historian Sir William Tarn, is decades past its academic sell-by date; but this wouldn't stop Oliver Stone recycling it too for his *Alexander*. Like Stone's *Alexander*, Scott's epic sends its hero eastward for parched desert battles, long marches and clichéd harem action. Bloom even gets a big black horse, Bucephalus-style. The one significant missing element is Hephaestion, conveniently lost in the translation from Ancient to Mediaeval.

Scott's departure didn't dent *Alexander*'s prospects. The casting of Leonardo DiCaprio as Alexander was announced shortly after Lurhmann's arrival; press releases named Nicole Kidman as Olympias in January 2003. The adventurous choice of director and star excited much interest among fans online. Ted Tally, the screenwriter on Demme's *Silence of the Lambs*, adapted the script from

Valerio Manfredi's *Alexander* trilogy. Throughout 2002 the project continued to be written up as the front-runner, likely to beat the Stone and Scorsese films into production.

The film subsequently trailed behind Stone's *Alexander*. A budget of $150m was reportedly secure and distribution deals were in place; but the start date for principal photography kept slipping. 9/11 and then the second Gulf War made the first choice of location, Morocco, look risky, prompting a relocation to Australia. Co-financer Universal, too, were hedging their bets between Luhrmann's *Alexander* and a possible Ridley Scott *Gladiator 2* – neither of which now appears to be going anywhere fast. By October 2004 it was all over ... for now, and depending on whom you asked. De Laurentiis was still talking it up in 2005 as a sure thing.

The 'best' *Alexander*: Christopher McQuarrie / Martin Scorsese

This project, the longest in gestation (since the early nineties) and now definitely dead in the water, was originated by screenwriter Christopher McQuarrie (*The Usual Suspects*). A leaked script of this embryonic production, by McQuarrie and Peter Buchman (*Jurassic Park III*), was highly praised by industry insiders. At first, McQuarrie was to have directed, with Matthew McConaughey as Alexander and Jude Law (allegedly McQuarrie's first choice for Alexander) as Hephaestion; the production would have shot in Morocco or Spain. The project was to have been produced by Warner Bros, who instead later became distributors for the Stone *Alexander*. When Warner pulled out, a German media company, Senator Entertainment, took on the production; Jude Law was tipped to be reinstated as McQuarrie's lead. Senator in turn dropped the project during a corporate reorganisation.

Leonardo DiCaprio replaced McConaughey as prospective star when the script was picked up by Initial Entertainment Group in

2001, with McQuarrie stepping aside for Scorsese, who had recently directed DiCaprio in *Gangs of New York*, as director. McQuarrie and co-writer Buchman remained with the project as associate producers. The Scorsese *Alexander* maintained the highest profile of all the Alexander projects throughout 2001, with publicity centring on the Scorsese / DiCaprio dream team (at a time when De Laurentiis had yet to settle on a director or a star). Scorsese, for his part, was busy talking up not just DiCaprio's Alexander-esque star quality but also his uncanny resemblance to Greek busts of Alexander. The film was still being hotly tipped for success in early 2002. Later that year, Scorsese and DiCaprio migrated to the Luhrmann project as executive producer and star respectively – another *Alexander* that would never quite come off. Their own *Alexander* had peaked too soon; and perhaps they had also had second thoughts about the story's problematic themes. With Luhrmann's film indefinitely on hold, Scorsese and DiCaprio banished their Alexander hangover with a lavish Howard Hughes biopic, *The Aviator* (2004); like Scott's *Kingdom of Heaven*, another *Alexander*-that-might-have-been. The Greek conqueror's towering achievements and ego kept their headline billing ('Imagine a Life without Limits'), while his problematic issues were nicely tidied away by a change of locale and love interest.

Passion of the *Alexander*: Mel Gibson

Not a film, but rather a high-budget ($120m), ten-episode TV series for the American HBO network, along the lines of their successful World War 2 epic *Band of Brothers*. This was one of two high-concept projects that Gibson was considering producing at the time via his Ikon production company; the other iron in the fire was an unlikely-sounding Aramaic-language biopic of Jesus. The script was to have been based on the well-regarded Alexander novels by Mary

Renault, *Fire from Heaven* (from which the series would have taken its name) and *The Persian Boy*. But Gibson lost interest, perhaps because of Renault's assertively gay-friendly take on her hero; and HBO shelved the series. Instead, with massive financial success, he filmed the Jesus biopic, *The Passion of the Christ*, choosing an ancient-world hero with a less problematic multiplex persona – at least in his estimation. Sadistic, monotonous and doctrinally hard-line, *Passion* received indifferent reviews and was widely accused of anti-Semitism; but its appeal to the previously underestimated Evangelical audience of the American heartlands brought it massive financial success and continues to sell DVDs as fast as they can be pressed. HBO, meanwhile, had settled on an ancient-world theme that would play equally well in the Mid-West – *Rome*, a lavishly produced, gritty exposé of the decadent Roman Republic filmed in collaboration with the BBC. A wonderful prospect for ancient history buffs, *Rome* was nonetheless a step backwards (from the brink?) on HBO's part; it even filmed at Rome's Cinecittà, the old Fascist-tinged stomping-ground of conventional toga epic from the silent age onwards.

Still, though, Alexander continued to move in mysterious ways. As late as mid-2003, Luhrmann and De Laurentiis were broadly hinting to the Australian press that Mel Gibson would come on board as Alexander's father, Philip. More recently, Gibson was rumoured to be producing Vin Diesel's *Hannibal* – Alexander re-pitched as heroic anti-Roman (*ergo* Christian-compatible) underdog, and not a Hephaestion in sight.

An *Alexander* for Hellas: T. Atcheson / Steven Mayas

Starring a near-unknown Steven Stratos, this wing-and-a-prayer Greek-expatriate *Alexander the Great* has a long and chequered pre-production history. In March 2003, director Atcheson and

screenwriter Boyd Rahier were briefly listed on IMDb as attached
to the Luhrmann production as co-director and –screenwriter; but
these and other attributions were removed in an April purge of
spurious credits. Elsewhere, Greek-Australian actor-writer-director
Steven Mayas (Eustratios Magias) was credited as screenwriter.
The movie was extensively plugged by Greek spammers on the
IMDb message boards for the Stone and Luhrmann projects, with
grandiose claims to carry 'the official endorsement and support
of the Greek Government and the Greek community internation-
ally' and the approval of the Onassis Foundation. The project
also claimed official endorsement from both the 2004 Athens
Olympics Committee and, with more concrete justification, the
hard-line nationalist Pan-Macedonian Association of the USA (www.
panmacedonian.info: 'True Macedonians Were and Are Greek'). The
sixty-one-page business plan for the film was for a time available
online from the Pan-Macedonians' website, and contained many
touching letters of support from Australian-Greek dioceses and
community organisations. It suggested, hopefully, that the Greek
Government might want to step in and pick up the tab. In the
meantime, patriotic Hellenes were invited to purchase shares in the
production at $100 a pop.

Also alleged were a budget of $120m, a late 2004 or early 2005
release, and the best Alexander look-alike as the film's star: the
publicity materials optimistically billed Stratos as a dead ringer for
the Alexander of the Issus mosaic. Also optimistic was the claimed
'potential to be the biggest grossing movie of all time'. Throughout,
the project in total has appeared to consist of the business plan,
a bare-bones website (www.alexanderthegreatmovie.com), a short
teaser of Stratos gazing at some hills and a Beverley Hills contact
address. Depending on one's source, the production company is /
was either 'American Films International' or, more recently, 'H. B. Inc
Productions', an outfit which appears to share the Pan-Macedonian

Association's ethnic-political agenda and whose CEO / President is Steven Mayas. According to the business plan, first unit photography will occur in Australia, with the second unit back home in Greece, where 'everything will be done *under the auspices of the ministry of culture*, virtually for free!' (original emphasis).

After all, it worked so well for *Atlas* ... The insistently upbeat rhetoric couldn't help but raise issues of credibility for the project, of which nothing new has been heard in a longish while. Indeed, it is hard to identify any objective likelihood, at any point since its inception, of the Atcheson / Mayas *Alexander the Great* coming to fruition – at least, in the obvious sense of actually becoming a film. Instead, and surely by design, its impact played out at the level of Alexander-discourse. Like the Shatner *Alexander*, it set up a far-reaching interference pattern which resonated with and altered the fabric of other projects – Stone's included – in surprising ways and out of all proportion to its resources. Scorsese's and Gibson's nearly-there blockbusters promised a generic Western Alexander with just the right amount of historiographical window-dressing, one perhaps barely distinguishable from the *Alexander* we finally saw in the cinema. Mayas' never-close microbrew epic aggressively pushed a very different and self-consciously Greek vision of Alexander, setting a deliberate collision course with adventurous (Lurhmann) and conservative (Stone) versions alike.

Not tonight, Hephaestion: sand, sex and star image

The Atcheson / Mayas project was not the only *Alexander* to see advantage in Australian locations; and the prospect that it might shoot alongside the much bigger Luhrmann production was intriguing, given the strongly phrased antipathy of its advocates to Luhrmann's (and indeed Stone's) supposed intentions. The criticisms expressed were in part a reaction to Luhrmann's image as a gay-friendly auteur; his film was dismissed with scathing *double entendre* as 'a fairy tale'. But H.B. Inc's ire was also fuelled by gay-positive comments fed to the film press by successive contenders for the starring role in Stone's picture. Mayas' patriotic Alexander was held up as the Greek community's right of reply to two enemies of historical truth who 'portray Alexander in a dark false light, as a savage, a barbarian, a drunk and an absolute [*sic*] homosexual. And above all, they portray Alexander as a Balkan and not a Greek!'

For Mayas and H.B. Inc, the true Alexander is a god-like 'hero' to the international Greek community – a transcendent, far-flung commonwealth united by racial purity and by the universality of Alexander's spirit. As spun by H.B. and the Pan-Macedonians, this global brotherhood is the sole and self-appointed custodian of Alexander's true meaning: it must keep the faith if it is to hold together. It would be literally 'destroyed' by a sufficiently influential Hollywood portrayal of the hero as ethnically or sexually suspect. Alexander must be a proper Greek and uphold proper Greek values – that is, the current values (conservatively glossed) of the expatriate community, including the Orthodox Church's compulsory heterosexuality. At the same time, this Orthodox Alexander has to be maintained as a poster boy for Greece's status as the bedrock of the Western Tradition, and particularly for democratic values. The happily pagan, drunkenly autocratic and sexually relaxed Alexanders of the Lurhmann and Stone projects (and of ancient literary accounts) were presented as unthinkable, unbearable – and *therefore* historically false. In this formulation, the fight to assert control over Alexander's meaning became a fight for the survival of the very idea of Greek identity. Mayas promised the world a 'true legendary Alexander' (*sic*): a paradox, but by no means a careless or naïve one. To non-believers, this formulation seems nonsensical; certainly the rhetoric is over-wrought. For the faithful, though, this promised Alexander was true *because* he was legendary, acceptable only insofar as his character and history complied with a pre-determined agenda of moral conservatism.

What's more, the grudge-bearing hardliners were far from alone in setting up a counterfactual Orthodox Alexander in their own image. Although their repeated characterisation of expatriate Greeks as Alexander's 'fanatic followers' had to be hot air, the church and community organisations which wrote in their support were every bit as insistent on Alexander's importance to the Hellenic ideal – and on the importance of cleaning up Alexander's act. Their Alexander is a genetically and culturally pure Greek, who conquers the world gently and for its own good. By this account, Alexander never really wanted to make war on anyone, as such; he was simply keen to share the benefits of Western-style democracy as widely and quickly as he could. We may not believe in the possibility of a 'true legendary Alexander' (or not this one); but he deserves to be taken seriously, if only because so many sincere and decent people feel they need him.

In comfortable retrospect, of course, the Pan-Macedonians' Slav-bashing rhetoric reads as laughably out of touch. Greece itself has cooled down considerably since its brief anti-Republic of Macedonia agitation a decade ago, leaving the business plan's denunciation of ethnic Slavs as 'savages' (and homosexual savages at that) looking increasingly anachronistic. Despite initial tensions and some ongoing awkwardness over nomenclature, enterprising Greeks rushed to invest in the development of their ex-Yugoslavian neighbour, following the lifting of their own government's cross-border embargo in 1995. In turn, the new Republic made significant compromises to Hellenic sensibilities, particularly the redesign of its flag (which initially bore the star emblem of Alexander's dynasty). We can reasonably dismiss the Pan-Macedonians' ethnic call to arms as the time-expired rhetoric of an oddball fringe; in particular, their claims of friends in high places were always hard to take seriously.

The expatriates' heterosexual panic over Alexander, however, is much closer to the party line – at least as reported in the international press. As early as November 1998, the Athens News Agency carried a story on the Greek Government's refusal to cooperate with Stone because of his stated intention to portray Alexander as bisexual; following *Alexander*'s release, the story flared up again in modified form, with Stone allegedly facing threats of court action from a coalition of eminent Greek lawyers in response to even the very coy homoerotic elements that made it to the final version. Stone's financers must have been delighted at this excellent free publicity. Reliable or not, though, this self-sustaining media controversy kept gay receptions of Alexander centre stage in popular responses to Stone's *Alexander* regardless of the intentions of the director – or the content of the film.

Were the hardliners right to panic? Alexander's enjoyment of both male and female sexual partners is as 'historical' as most of the Alexander-factoids of the modern historical / biographical tradition, although the evidence is limited; the issue just didn't excite ancient Greek writers, who seem to have taken relationships with Hephaestion and others more or less as read. Modern popular receptions have glossed these same-sex relationships as a gay or bisexual identity. The process began with the gay community's recuperation of Alexander as a famous historical role model alongside (among others) Socrates. This explicitly politicised subcultural appropriation was then subsumed at an unthreatening soundbite level into mainstream popular culture, in part thanks to the popularity of Mary Renault's 1970s Alexander novels and particularly *The Persian Boy* (1980). Renault's own version proved too much for Gibson and HBO, but the three other front-running *Alexanders* competed for publicity via a dialogue with the press which took a Big Gay Alexander as a given. Responding to the glut of film projects still in the running in autumn 2001, The New York Daily News characterised the historical

Alexander as 'the gay empire-builder', while the UK's *Guardian* went for a similar potted history: 'the first bisexual action hero'. Richard Burton had played his Alexander more or less straight, at a time when commercial cinema was compelled to be coy; but the new Hollywood hopefuls saw positive advantage in courting the pink dollar. Alexander's new anything-that-moves sexuality became just another arena for Hollywood one-upmanship, as the main players jostled for media and fan attention with carefully timed press releases. Each *Alexander* in turn claimed the strongest script, the biggest budget, the most famous stars, the most uncanny look-alike – and (Mayas excepted) the most 'authentically' bisexual action hero. Stone, Luhrmann and, while he remained in the running, Scorsese played high-stakes movie poker, progressively upping the ante. We will never know how much of it was empty bluff; Stone's finished film was strikingly vague about Alexander's same-sex relationships, but his rivals were by then seemingly out of the game. While they remained at the table, their currency was star image – Alexander's, Cruise's (an early Stone pick), DiCaprio's, Farrell's, and the directors' own public personae as auteurs.

Often it was hard to tell where one star ended and another began. Leonardo DiCaprio was written up as 'king of the ancient world', reworking the dialogue of his *Titanic* character. (The 'king of the world' line had already become a pop-culture soundbite thanks to *Titanic*'s maverick director James Cameron, who recycled it in his Oscar acceptance speech.) His personal fan base dubbed his future Alexander 'Leo the Great' and 'DiCaprio the Great'. By way of contrast, Heath Ledger, briefly a contender for Stone's Alexander, receded from view once publicists had worked out that there was no interesting way of linking his star image to Alexander's own. (Ironically, he would subsequently out-gay all the rival Alexanders in Ang Lee's *Brokeback Mountain* (2005).) Farrell's cultivated persona, by contrast, could be sold not just through Alexander's star image but Burton's too (wild Celt, hard partier, ladies' man). If Alexander is just another role, so too, perhaps, is DiCaprio, Cruise, or Farrell; or the director's own role as showman and advocate. Scorsese's intentions for *Alexander*, for instance, were sold to the press as 'passionate' – hyping the great director's latest ancient-world project via the publicity storm that surrounded *The Last Temptation of Christ*. (Gibson's Damascene conversion from his Alexander miniseries to *The Passion of the Christ* closes the rhetorical circle with inadvertent neatness.) Scorsese was able to sell Alexander to the world (until the project stalled) by merging him into Leo's own star image, again assimilating contemporary beefcake to supposedly authenticating ancient mise-en-scène: 'There's a bust of Alexander, and it bears an amazing resemblance. He had great charisma. Someone called him the first superstar.' Starring 'pretty boy debutant' Leo as Alexander, or (ditto) Alexander as Leo? Either way, the public was and is hungry to buy.

H. B. Inc.'s *Alexander* pitched itself to a rather different public but was essentially playing the same game. The big difference was in its choice of which star image to bring into play. Steven Stratos would play Alexander, but he was never the *star*. Instead, Greek ethnicity would star as Alexander – or Alexander as Greek ethnicity. Authentic Greeks would inevitably deliver an authentic Alexander because his blood lived on in them; race was destiny and history, and now it would become cinema. Supporting roles could safely be distributed among established Hollywood players: the business plan optimistically pencilled in a dream team of character actors with strong audience appeal. (Some of these prospective casting decisions are bracingly original; as Aristotle, Christopher Walken could have changed our ideas of philosophy forever.) Alexander's own star image, however, had to be kept safe from foreign contamination. Stratos was ideally cast: an unknown bit-player, he would bring nothing extraneous to the role. His performance was intended as a blank space onto which Greeks everywhere could project their shared myth of a founding hero who blazes the trail for expatriate communities worldwide, conquering as far as India and – given a few more years of life – surely Australia too. But the film was additionally intended to deliver closure to Greeks abroad, to offer a vicarious Homeric *nostos* or homecoming to the mother country as conquering heroes. The $100 shareholders would not only see their investments repaid many times over:

> They will also be considered as national heroes, by the international Greek community. An *Alexander Monument* will be built in Greece, where all the names of those involved in this project, who were responsible in helping *preserve the Hellenic history*, will have *their names engraved for all time!* They will be remembered as those who fought to save and protect our historic heritage ... (original emphases)

The Pan-Macedonians' *Alexander* was pitched as a patriotic defence by Greece's citizen hoplites against a superficially stronger barbarian invader – a cinematic Thermopylae, pitting a home-grown *300 Spartans* against the communist-inspired hordes of Stone and Luhrmann (and beating back *Gates of Fire* while it was there). The sensible money was always on the hordes; but then, the Persians were probably getting good odds in the fifth century BC. Perhaps it will even be made in some form one day.

'To the strongest': Oliver Stone, *Alexander* (2004)

Oliver Stone's *Alexander* emerged as the leading contender no earlier than 2003, with the commencement of location filming following years of seemingly endless deferrals. Stone (*Platoon, JFK*) claimed to have been intent on making an *Alexander* since at least the mid-nineties; but claims of this kind are an established part of the publicity game, and pre-filming word of mouth was decidedly mixed. Stone hinted heavily that the plot would revolve around his own *JFK*-style conspiracy theory, explaining Alexander's early death as a political assassination; classicists and other pedants were relieved to find this aspect soft-pedalled in the final cut. Industry gossip alleged that Stone approached Gore Vidal (an old toga-movie hand) as a potential scriptwriter but was rebuffed; in the end, in a probably unconscious imitation of Rossen, the director wrote his own version. There were worries, too, over the casting of Alexander (first Heath Ledger, then Colin Farrell) – for reasons that by now should be fairly clear.

But most of the worries centred around Stone, and not just among cinephiles. Would he traduce the 'true legendary Alexander' in whom so many communities and interest groups claimed a controlling interest? Alexander's expatriate Greek devotees were certainly on edge. In one strange attempt at a spoiling tactic, they re-jigged the Vidal rumour and claimed that Stone had been briefly considered as a potential director for their feature, only to be turned down on grounds of political incompatibility; we might wonder whether he ever knew he was in the running. In the end, and in part surely because of their successful high-profile agitation, *Alexander* would give them little to worry about. Concern was also voiced among another, equally insistent special interest group, the professional classics community – but their fears were rather more quickly soothed by the highly publicised appointment of an eminent Oxford classicist, Robin Lane Fox, as historical adviser. Lane Fox's appointment was an inspired solution; at a stroke, it placated all the aggrieved parties. The historian's insistence in his best-selling biography that Alexander's family was essentially Greek had long endeared him to Greek fans of Alexander – and in particular to the Pan-Macedonians. (Carefully edited Lane Fox-isms are quoted liberally in their press releases.) It didn't even cost Stone a cent; his adviser agreed to work gratis, in exchange for a posting in the front rank of each cavalry charge. (Through documentaries and interviews, this much-noised freebie deal itself became key pre-release PR for *Alexander*.)

Unexpectedly, then, and against all Stone's established form, this was an *Alexander* that went out of its way to avoid frightening the horses – a cautious, conservative and thoughtful epic, with a more serious claim than most to (some kind of) historical fidelity. Yet it opened to largely negative notices and did miserably at the box office. How did this nobly intentioned and intelligently supported project turn into one of the biggest cinematic disasters of recent years?

The press and other mainstream popular media queued up to murder *Alexander* (as cinema and as 'history') before a wide public, and academic reviewers too have put the boot in at a more specialised level; I see little mileage in reiterating these widely distributed criticisms. My own personal suspicion is that the film Stone accidentally ended up making is not so much his (allegedly) long-cherished *Alexander* as it is the yet more interminably deferred follow-up to the film on which the director cut his teeth as a writer of ancient-world epic: *King Conan*, sequel to leaden, macho slugfest *Conan the Barbarian*. The similarities are there to be pointed out and the comparison can explain a certain amount of what is wrong with *Alexander* (suddenly John Milius' Van Damme *Alexander* no longer sounds quite so outlandish); but casual Stone-bashing of this kind, fun though it is for a while, gets us nowhere terribly interesting. Instead, I suggest, we can make better critical use of *Alexander's* problems by placing them in context. The film's profound difficulties of pacing and coherence begin with its anxiety to massage the (often mutually incompatible) concerns of the special interest groups with a declared stake in Alexander's reception, scholars and chauvinists alike. The nods to Alexander's expatriate Greek devotees are clear enough, whether in the dreamy Vangelis soundtrack, largely recycled from *Chariots of Fire*, or in Alexander's excruciatingly coy relationship with Hephaestion. (The day I saw *Alexander*, the cinema collapsed into laughter – a welcome break from the yawns – at Roxane's 'Do you love that man?'). In Alexander's high-minded 'dream' of spreading civilised Greek values worldwide, Stone not only panders to academics guiltily nostalgic for Sir William Tarn's gentlemanly 1950s certainties (Lane Fox surely among them); he also summons up the saintly Orthodox Alexander, invoked, as we have seen, by a range of expatriate interest groups as a prototype for the modern Greek diaspora. Alexander's Greatness is insistently Greekness too. Hamming his way through the closing voice-over as he waits for the pay cheque to clear, Anthony Hopkins (a piece of casting recycled from another, non-starting *Alexander*) declaims that Alexander was '*Megalexandros* – the greatest Alexander of all'. *Megalexandros* is indeed authentic Greek for 'Alexander the Great' (not 'greatest'), but it is not *ancient* Greek; Alexander is *Megalexandros* only in later receptions. In fact, it is not until the Romans appropriate Alexander as a role-model that he becomes 'the Great', an epithet which the Greeks subsequently borrow back to feed their own cultural nostalgia. Like all the other Alexanders, *Megalexandros* is just another reception – a wishful phantom, a cipher onto which interested parties can project their own concerns and priorities. (It is worth noting in passing that one of the main Pan-Macedonian agitators for the Mayas *Alexander* signed off his internet postings as 'Megalexandros'.)

As ever, then, and despite the finest scholarly fire-proofing that money can (or in this case – even better – couldn't) buy, Rome leaks in from the edges via the other Alexanders – rival contenders and previous receptions alike. Looming particularly large is Rossen's original epic, of which Stone's supposedly very personal film turns out to be practically a scene-for-scene remake, in much the same way as Scott's *Gladiator* retells *Fall of the Roman Empire*. If anything, *Alexander* is a closer match to its prototype. As Hopkins' gouty Ptolemy ticks off sacked cities in his dictated memoirs, we move in on a pretty mosaic map of Alexander's eastern conquests, very like Rossen's; again, the place-names are all in Latin. The blond fright-wig, the attention-seeking rhetoric, the cast padded with slumming Shakespeareans, above all, the leaden pacing; it's all here, minus Rossen's token arthouse stylings. (Impressionistic montage is replaced by plodding voiceover as a vehicle for infodump; was montage perhaps another casualty of reception and spin, as Stone laboured to distance his project from 'arty' competing representations?) Despite good bought-in scholarly advice, some of Rossen's difficulties of costuming and mise-en-scène carry across as well – and grow in the re-telling. The map mosaic is a good example: bigger, flashier and with even more Latin than the original. Torchlit caveman Philip has not only lumbered straight out of Rossen's picture, apparently still clad in the same woolly bath-mat – he has picked up a gallery of thrillingly brutish cave paintings along the way (a scene savaged by reviewers). Some of *Alexander*'s wider problems with mise-en-scène (which invariably turn into problems with narrative: the set-dressing tells us how to read the scene) are less to do with Rossen than with generic toga-movie contamination. The red cloaks of Alexander's generals can't help signifying Rome; legionaries were surely the last thing on the costume designers' minds, but within larger patterns of pop-culture reception the visual subtext is inescapable from an audience perspective. Stone not only chooses to cast a fey Celt as Alexander (swapping in Irishman Farrell for Welsh Burton) – he makes all his 'Macedonian' leads put on a picturesque Oirish accent to hammer home their marginal Greek identity. (Farrell had discarded his own in pursuit of an American career; the lower-class burr he affects for *Alexander* irritated the hell out of my Irish companion.) Stone's point is sound, and the use of accent is a very economical way of putting it across; but it's also another locus of contamination, both from the toga movie and from *Alexander*'s own filmic prehistory. Whip-cracking Romans have been delivering clipped British RP to oppressed, all-American Christians since Cecil B. de Mille invented the convention in his thirties epics. The choice of a Celtic regional accent ties *Alexander* to genre nadirs *The Robe* and *Cleopatra* via the performances of Rossen's Alexander, Richard Burton. ('Stand back, rejoice, Marc Antony will save the day!') We have come full circle to the problems that sank *Atlas*, *Colossus* and *Helen of Troy* in ch.1. Commitment, professionalism and even, in Stone's case, a well-earned reputation as one of cinema's great radicals were not and are not enough in themselves to move the *peplum* on. Stone's film can never escape the past it denies.

Nor can it break free of the participatory Alexander-discourse of modern popular culture, which continually insists on reading (any) *Alexander* against points of reference of its own choosing – often productively so. By accident and (in passing) by design, Stone's epic emerges as a kind of anti-Shatner *Alexander*. A straight-faced, heavy-handed, completely humourless slog of a film, it substitutes pasted-in exposition for narrative drive and punches well below its budget visually. It also, despite its best and most debilitating intentions, ended up offending at least one special interest group in ways that no-one had anticipated – the Zoroastrians, a very ancient religious community who saw their sacred emblems traduced by *Alexander*'s insensitive mise-en-scène. (Clearly they should have got online sooner, or threatened an *Alexander* of their own.) But the bearers of Alexander's flame loved it – or at least queued up to express polite approval. On the off-chance that anyone out there was listening, British classicists in particular rallied behind Lane Fox and, with less fanfare, Lloyd Llewellyn-Jones, the film's costume advisor, as guarantors of *Alexander*'s respectability as a true – or true enough – historical narrative. In part, this stemmed from an understandable wish to avoid embracing the media cliché of the ancient historian as dusty pedant. (Who cares if Angelina Jolie's frock is all wrong – the chitons are fine!) In part, too, it was relief and even gratitude: things genuinely had been done that little bit more 'authentically' across the board this time, and not just on the level of mise-en-scène. (Look! A real phalanx, with proper sarissae!) It's easy to feel sympathy with these impulses; but the rush to exculpate *Alexander* also reflected the economics of the lecture hall. The critics had hung *Alexander* out to dry, but if it could be talked up as a worthwhile enterprise, it would fit nicely into any number of easy-to-teach, recruitment-boosting 'classics and film' courses, allowing Rossen's film an honourable retirement from its duties as lecture-room staple. (So what if the cinema cut wasn't great – the DVD version will fix everything!) Again, it's easy to see the dons' side of the picture. The classics debate also laid bare the prejudices and politics of the academic job market. Colosseum expert Kathleen Coleman had publicly distanced herself from the historical mess of *Gladiator*, a film she was (by her own very interesting account) unable to save from Ridley Scott's audience-savvy showman enthusiasms; but Alexander expert Robin Lane Fox was clearly made of sterner stuff. He had old-school rigour, all the right dead languages and, most importantly, *gravitas* on his side; in short, he was academic aristocracy and it was no wonder Stone had seen sense. Along the way, too, UK classicists' carefully worded apologetics for Stone's film made all the right noises about the state (and status) of ancient history at Lane Fox's Oxford – coincidentally, the dream ticket for career-minded UK classicists. Ancient-world academia turned out to be just another squabbling subculture, spilling its office politics in print and on the Web for the entertainment of anyone who cared to pay attention. Stone's habit of consultation didn't make the experts any more 'objective' than the next interest group. (Was Ptolemy's voiceover the cornerstone of Stone's vision for *Alexander*, or a bungled after-thought? It depended which expert you asked.)

Lane Fox himself, meanwhile, had entered a magically rejuve-nating second adolescence. Leading the charge and looking over the daily rushes, he was finally confirmed in what he had said all those years back in his 1973 biography of Alexander. Only a chap of his own all-round calibre (gentleman and scholar, polymath, rider to hounds) could hope to understand what had made the real Alexander tick – and Stone was man enough to accept this. So, too, was his youthful male lead. In Lane Fox's terribly revealing offi-cial guide to the film, *The Making of Alexander*, the method-acting Farrell becomes an unconscious channel for the spirit of Alexander, a mediumistic role underwritten by his impetuous youth and more particularly by (I'm not kidding) his fey Irish blood; he brings Lane Fox face to face at last with the flesh-and-blood yearnings of the man behind the texts:

> 'He was young, but I see him always with an old soul' … I began to feel I should have talked more to this film-Alexander before writing my history … 'I've had to become what you never dared to be,' he found himself saying to his father's relics.

But if Farrell is at times possessed by Alexander's ghost, Stone *is* an Alexander: a mercurial battle-commander ('famous for sudden improvisations') and all-round Renaissance Man ('Caravaggio'), even, explicitly, a new Dionysus. And Lane Fox gets to hob-nob with his lifetime hero. The pair become heroic symposiasts, bonded late-night drinking companions in the manner of Alexander and his Companions. 'We talked more personally, of our schooling … When the wine came, could he pour it steadily? But it was I who was the more exhausted'. Lane Fox's agenda in writing the official guide is explicitly and conservatively pedagogic, glossing Stone's epic via authoritative annotation as an ancient history primer for the masses; and inevitably, the subtexts come bubbling through (Addington Symonds would have had a field day). The historian even coaches Stone in *kottabos*, the ancient Greek drinking game celebrating same-sex desire. Through his hero-worship of the director, and quite unselfconsciously, the historian burnishes and elaborates his own very personal fashioning of Alexander as – to simplify only a little – an Etonian Hemingway, a beautiful (but also tough and capable) senior boy on whom he has a lifetime schoolboy crush. When Oliver / Alexander asks Lane Fox to finish his history prep for him, the hero-worshipping historian finds complete personal fulfilment. And why shouldn't he? Lane Fox's old-school insistence on an objective and fact-bounded 'real' Alexander ends up delivering a passionately *personal* Alexander, a larger-than-life and richly imagined persona that leaves the interest groups' rival characterisations looking tired and generic. It's a paradox that, viewed against the warring Alexanders of contemporary reception, makes a strange kind of sense; and if there is irony in this outcome, it's of a salutary and empowering (not to say heart-warming) kind. Via subculture, we can and should take Greece personally. If Alexander is to be good for anything at all these days, he should at least be able to make an old man very happy.

Alexander's legacy matters; he remains a name to conjure with, a name that is all the more powerful because we cannot pin it down to a single, agreed meaning. As Greek history's big-name star, he stands as an exemplar for 'real' Greece on film. His tantalising potential makes him hot property – and often, as we have seen, too hot to handle. As the second millennium wound up, Alexander exerted a renewed fascination over the stars and auteurs who would assume his mantle as 'king of the world'; but he appalled the studios and moneymen, who faced the prospect of a wasteful and chancy epic succession. Much the same anxieties confronted Alexander's ancient successors. Heroic comradeship with the former god-king was their only claim to power in the short term, but he was a dangerous and double-edged role model for would-be dynastic rulers: a world conqueror (who inevitably put his successors in the shade), a drunkard, a queer, a tyrant with barbarism in his blood. Alexander was a mixed blessing, and even a necessary evil. Hollywood might have found him a less daunting subject over the years if he had a little *less* star quality. Even the expatriate Greeks who claimed Alexander as their patron and prototype found themselves inadvertently rehashing ancient *Roman* receptions at every turn. Alexander as peace-loving world conqueror is a soft-filter Augustus straight out of Virgil's *Aeneid*; and Orthodox agitation over pretty-boy stars and sexually suspect characterisations directly mirrors the anxieties over the Greek body beautiful and gymnasium culture which we find expressed in so many Roman authors. (This is a realisation which we might productively read back into any number of modern receptions and receptions-of-receptions, casting a new light on – among others – the insistent camping-up of *Troy* in the reviews.) The 'fanatic followers' were also faced with an obvious and awkward question. If Alexander's story and spirit belong to modern Greeks everywhere; if a Greek film of Alexander is really nothing more complex than a patriotic drama-documentary, then where are all the Greek *Alexanders*?

Where, too, were *Alexander*'s Hollywood Successors? In *Gladiator*'s aftermath, the new wave of multiplex *pepla* was pitched as a renaissance for the classical epic. New understandings and technologies – and, crucially, Greek rather than Roman themes – would enable a genre moribund since the early 1960s to achieve its true potential at last, moving on from the tired, pious clichés of the *Quo Vadis* era. It's worth remembering that practically the same evangelical sales pitch had pushed reception studies itself back in the early 1990s, when it was touted as the saviour of classical studies (and the overdue Death of Classics); that any-day-now deconstruction of the Western Canon somehow never quite came about. If the façade of optimism for the *pepla* cracked post-*Troy*, the aftermath of *Alexander* seemed to leave ancient Greece with no options at all – at least in mainstream cinema. But Greece may yet surprise us. Certainly it keeps opening up options for reception, pushing us onward and away from the new-for-old canons and certainties (*Quo Vadis*, *Ben-Hur*) that had threatened to turn it into just another 'Classical Tradition' course. Above all, the new 'Wars of the Successors' are a salutary reminder that receptions of ancient Greece in popular culture remain unpredictable, because that's the way reception – and popular culture – work. As authored, 'closed' receptions of ancient Greece, as 'films in themselves', *Troy* and *Alexander* fail to move the game on; in fact, they fall into some very old habits indeed. But that is not the end of their story. The rest of the story is 'open': it will be written by popular culture itself, actively and continuously, in ten thousand smaller narratives of collaboration, revision, co-option and contestation. Fans, subcultures and special interest groups will continue to war for the succession, a war that can now have no end. Among these groups are the academics, who once professed to own or at least to direct the story's meaning; but ownership and control will increasingly move beyond the reach of any one subculture, away from the draughty old High Culture pedestal that got ancient Greece into its present fix, and that's all to the good. It is happening out there right now; and this, for me, is where the real grit and interest of reception kick in.

And now we finally have a film that plays to this dynamic. In 2007, we dined in classics hell.

4

2007:
IT'S RAINING MEN

The Pelopenessian War [sic] is not over by a long shot and that is why you have never heard this before. Athens has won in the Universities ... The Universities are filled with effeminates and desk bound urbans who hate manliness, virility and warriors

Greek-expatriate IMDb spammer, March 2007

On the contrary, we *love* warriors – but we can never eat just one. Three news items came my way as the first edition went to press in late 2006.

The first closed the loop on the Pan-Macedonians. Funded by their donations, and inaugurated in 1999, a modern shrine to Alexander – the *Alexandreion* (*Alexandrion Doma*, 'Alexandrios Building') – was nearing completion at Litohoro among the foothills of Mount Olympus. This international cultural centre is, or will become, a 'perpetual beacon for research and enlightenment of the historical work and insurmountable deeds of Alexander'; presently its doors open every four years for an international conference at which visiting cadres of the Macedonian Youth (yes, really) are inducted in the 'scientific truth' of the legendary commander. At the same time, and not too far down the road, a rival cult had also been busy. The Chicago-based Alexander the Great Foundation, Inc. had kicked off a minor media circus in 2002–3 with plans for an

Alexander-sanctuary of its own: an educational theme-park centred on a 260-foot, Mount Rushmore-style portrait carved into the face of Mount Kerdyllion. Abandoned in the face of protests by local archaeologists and environmentalists, this mega-Alexander would have gazed out towards Mount Athos, famously the never-used canvas on which the ancient Greek sculptor Dinocrates had hoped to carve an even larger Alexander of his own. Business as usual, then, for the 'true legendary' hero.

Meanwhile, the Pan-Macedonian Association continued its mission to counter the lies of Slav barbarians ('It is our Sacred Duty to continue our struggle for the rights of Macedonia. History demands it') and induct us in the mysteries of Alexander, precursor of Christ (foretold by the Prophets!) and 'vehicle of God' in spreading Greek culture to be the fertile seed-bed of the Christian faith.

The second item remains unresolved. Always an unlikely successor, the teen-angst soap *Alexander the Great from Macedonia*, aka *Macedonia's Alexander the Great*, was touted for worldwide release by the end of the year, under yet another Herculean alias: *Young Alexander the Great*. At the time of publication (Summer 2008), the website carries a bare-bones trailer (echoes of the Mayas *Alexander*) and still insists the film will be released in 2006, perhaps by firing it backwards through time in Bill and Ted's telephone booth. Shooting locations were, are, or will be Egypt and Greece itself – always a good sign, *Atlas* fans – and the director is Jalal Mehri, a Lebanese martial-arts specialist 'known to his admirers as Beirut's Steven Segal'. As with so many Alexanders, this one's still out there somewhere, or claims to be. Meanwhile, alas, Baz Lurhmann's *Alexander* was definitely dead; his Olympias, Nicole Kidman, will take the lead in his forthcoming national epic, *Australia* (2008).

The third, of course, had come from leftfield and would soon conquer at the box-office: 300, the mostly-CGI adaptation of Miller's graphic novel.

'Prepare for glory!': 300 (2006)

Xerxes. Yours is a fascinating tribe. There is much our cultures
could share.
Leonidas. Haven't you noticed? We've been sharing our culture
with you all morning.
Blair. On the contrary, we respect Iran as an ancient civilisation,
as a nation with a proud and dignified history.

Released worldwide in March 2007, 300 lived in interesting timing.
In the domestic US market its reception was inseparable from international politics. Critics and audiences immediately pegged the film
as the analogy *du jour*, a cartoonishly crude pretext for anything and
everything Bush's generals might feel like doing to Iran. Anti-war
liberals did their best to push an earnest against-the-grain reading
– plucky Iraqi/Spartan insurgents resist corrupt US/Persian imperialism! – but no-one was really buying. Leonidas' heroes just *so
obviously were* Pentagon hawks, and any Spartan who wasn't (the
Ephors, Theron) was quickly shown up as a traitorous, cheese-eating
surrender monkey:

Gorgo. Freedom is not free at all. It is paid for in blood.

Famously inscribed on the Korean War Veterans' Memorial, 'Freedom
Is Not Free' has since become the omnipresent cliché of hard-line
American conservatism and has taken on particular currency in
the ongoing War against Terror. T-shirts with the slogan do brisk
business among Guantanamo guards; Camp Delta's own motto is
'Honor Bound to Defend Freedom'. European audiences, of course,
recognised Gorgo's slogan primarily from *Team America: World Police*
(2004), the satirical epic from the creators of *South Park*, where its
use is parodic – but then, Europe is further to the left and keener
on cheese. Back home, and without evident irony, Warner's synopsis

declared that the Spartans (always such staunch fans of representative government) were 'drawing a line in the sand for democracy'. Audiences weren't left in much doubt *whose* sand that was likely to be.

But the film was structured and packaged to accommodate ironic readings too – if only because irony outsells patriotism in a domestic market in two minds over a protracted foreign war. Within the film, Miller's editorial voice became just *one* voice (albeit the only one we got to hear) – Dilios', the surviving Spartan sent by Leonidas to rally the Greeks against the invader. By recasting the graphic novel's captions as Dilios' excitable campfire pep-talk, Snyder and his collaborators bracketed Miller's ultra-conservative revisionism and offered a get-out for 300's homo-, xeno- and liberal-phobia – if you were inclined to accept one, and not all audiences were. (Sex columnist Dan Savage nailed the film's sexual and racial politics: 'Homophobic? It's Ann Coulter on a meth binge ... George Bush is going to blow a load in his pants when he sees this movie.') The publicity machine played all the angles as well. For every patriotic sales pitch there was a cast-and-crew interviewee ready to talk up the harmless camp ('There were so many scenes where if you changed the tone three per cent one way or the other, it became hilarious') or plug 300 as a zestfully innocent cartoon. The implicit point, later made tediously explicit by countless online apologists, was that you'd be dumb to read a mere comic – by definition, kids' stuff (although the film was 'R') – as political allegory. In a canny and much-quoted formulation, the director Zack Snyder called his own film an exercise in 'hysterical weirdness'; no arguing with that, but it handily pulled the plug on reading for ideology.

Outside the US, meanwhile, the film *was* international politics – particularly in Iran (where the banned film was extensively analysed by the official media) and the UK. Building on the US liberal reaction, leftist critics panned its politics: the *Guardian* frothed at 'an uncritical reflection of neocon foreign policy filmed at a time when that crazed ideology was at its most influential ... a video war-game'; *Socialist Worker* warned the party faithful against a 'rank cesspool of racism, sexism, homophobia and "freedom-loving" pro-war propaganda [which] continues to spew the right-wing politics of its creator [Miller]'. Even so, most UK critics in particular saw the funny side, bought the have-it-both-ways sales pitch and – predictably – talked up the camp value.

The Iranian line was stronger. 300 was the end-product of a sustained American conspiracy to destroy their culture:

> American cultural officials thought they could get mental satisfaction by plundering Iran's historic past and insulting this civilisation. Following the Islamic Revolution in Iran, Hollywood and cultural authorities in the US initiated studies to figure out how to attack Iranian culture. Certainly, the recent movie is a product of such studies.
>
> Javad Shamqadri, cultural advisor to Iranian president
> Mahmoud Ahmadinejad

Iran wasn't simply Persia's geopolitical heir, it *was* Persia – one unbroken civilisation through the millennia. Misrepresenting the one was a direct attack on the other – just as the unorthodox Alexander-projects of godless Hollywood had threatened some communities' idea of Greek identity. (Iran's great enemy of the 1980s–90s, Ba'athist Iraq, had set up a similar relationship to its own ancient past: Saddam Hussein had declared himself the new Nebuchadnezzar and rebuilt Babylon as a monument to his own regime.) As it happened, Iranians had been upset by *Alexander* too, not for the religious reasons of the Zoroastrians but because Stone had presented Persia's fall to Alexander as a narrative footnote in a phoned-in Anthony Hopkins voice-over. *Alexander* had clearly been an early product of the conspiracy, but 300 was its climax

– a *Triumph of the Will* for the twenty-first century. Iran's Minister of Culture declared it 'an insult to the entire Iranian nation'; its Academy of Arts drafted a UNESCO declaration equating the film's cultural vandalism to the desecration of a world heritage site; a Presidential advisor called it 'psychological warfare ... plundering Iran's historic past and insulting this civilisation'. The national media reflected and amplified a pervasive and politically convenient moral panic. (A Tehran blogger quipped: 'for the first time in a long while, taxi drivers are shaking their fists in agreement when the state news comes on'.) Not having seen the forbidden film – or pretending not to have seen it; the streets of Tehran were awash with bootlegs – made one all the more qualified to a share of the outrage. TV evening news detected a Zionist conspiracy and 'a new front in the war against Iran'. The print media concurred that 300 was a Trojan Horse for American militarist aggression, propaganda designed to sell the message 'that Iran, which is in the Axis of Evil now, has for long been the source of evil and modern Iranians' ancestors are the ugly murderous dumb savages you see in 300'. (Well, at least they weren't homosexual Slavs.)

As with *Alexander* and the Greek diaspora, some of the most outspoken criticisms came from self-identified Persians overseas; the response of expatriate Iranian bloggers in the US became an international news item in its own right. (And at least one expat Greek took umbrage at Persia muscling in on their trademark history-demands-it schtick: 'the fight for freedom and democracy is in our DNA ... Bitch ass persians raising a flag of a country they escaped pffffft ...') But the film became international politics far more literally on 23 March 2007. This was 300's UK release date; it was also the day on which Iranian naval forces detained at gunpoint fifteen British service personnel after they had boarded a merchant ship at a disputed location in or near Iraqi waters.

Persian emissary. This is blasphemy! This is madness!
Leonidas. Madness? This is Sparta!
Blair. Throughout, we have taken a measured approach: firm but calm, not negotiating but not confronting either.

300 and the detention story instantly became each other's subtexts, usually implicit but always present. (The parallelism was drawn out much more explicitly in online discussion forums; on the IMDb, breaking news generated long and heated exchanges as to whether this proved 300 had been propaganda for invading Iran all along.) The Iranian armed forces' seizure of the British crew as trespassers had set up a crude but effective morality-play in which President Ahmadinejad would show the world who the real 'murderous dumb savages' were. Iran/Persia was the voice of justice and mercy, pardoning its enemies ('we want peace and security for all people') and sending them home as a birthday present to the world:

> On the occasion of the birth anniversary of the great prophet of Islam, and on the occasion of Easter and Passover, I would like to announce that the great nation of Iran, while it is entitled to put the British military personnel on trial, has pardoned these 15 sailors and gives their release to the people of Britain as a gift.

The British response played to the same double-coded script. Blair's press statements engaged face-on with the shaken fists of those Iranian taxi drivers at 300's 'insult' to Persian culture – all the while studiously avoiding naming the culprit:

> To the Iranian people, I would simply say this: We bear you no ill will. *On the contrary, we respect Iran as an ancient civilisation, as a nation with a proud and dignified history.* And the disagreements that we have with your government we hope to resolve peacefully through dialogue.

But invoking 300 as the analogic elephant in the room could play in ways neither side could control. Ahmadinejad's presentation of gifts at the release of the service personnel was clearly meant to be read as PR for his statesmanship – a fertile homeland magnanimous in victory. But his proffered bags of pistachios cast him as a decidedly cheap date compared to the proffered jewels and harems of Xerxes' tyrannical largesse:

Every desire – every happiness you can imagine – every pleasure your fellow Greeks and your false gods have denied you – I will grant you. For I am kind.

And the outraged response of the British press to the perceived lack of moral fibre of its Marines may have explicitly invoked the spirit of Dunkirk, but couldn't help playing out against the pervasive media presence of 300's neocon hysterics, to say nothing of scarily literal US audience responses to the film as a call to arms against Islam:

[300] has awoken the average American to the importance of sacrifice on a personal level ... the voice of a nation is growing stronger ... Just for the record. My country, my family and my neighbors can have my blood right now.

'Only the hard and strong may call themselves Spartans' ... Then again, how could we be sure this was a *real* patriot? What if it was some giggling kid, 'trolling' the discussion boards to kick up liberal outrage for laughs?

'Our bees will blot out the sun': 300 and the YouTube generation

Fan, audience and critical responses to *Troy* and *Alexander* had been shaped to an unprecedented extent by the newly ubiquitous interactivity of the Web. In the two intervening years, the interactive dynamic had evolved; 300's reception worldwide was inseparable from YouTube. The classic (if not clichéd) internet success story, YouTube was founded in a garage in February 2005; twenty-one months later, search-and-content giant Google paid $1.65bn for it. As most readers will by now know, YouTube streams video content provided by corporate partners and private individuals. The service and content are free of charge; the site's business model is based on advertising to the hundreds of millions of casual browsers (billions, by the time you read this) who watch video clips on it every single day. More serious users interact by uploading content, swapping favourites (emailed YouTube links swiftly became the ubiquitous new office humour) and rating each others' clips. These home-made short films range from cute-pet scenes shot on mobile phones to semi-professional op-ed segments. Other content is professionally produced, including television news from all around the world and, soon, every music video ever made.

YouTube, in other words, has become a microcosm of the Web in all its variety – discounting the porn (which is banned), and if one can use the term 'microcosm' to describe a site which already contains far more content than the whole Web did just a couple of years ago. It's also the immediate go-to place for a new generation of mass-cultural consumers wanting to find or express opinions on any new film. Official trailers and teasers are instantly available, but unofficial recycling of segments from the finished film invariably follows within a day of its release. Often these piratical acts of bricolage are satirical, recutting the movie and adding a new soundtrack to turn it into a thirty-second critique of its perceived agendas and subtexts. Fans had been doing this kind of thing for decades, including online, but always within and for their own alternative-media subcultures. YouTube takes video parody into the mainstream and turns it into a mass-culture commodity every bit as pervasive as the 'official' media it recycles.

Type '300' into YouTube's search box – as any new-generation consumer now will, *as a first resort*, in seeking to find or share opinions on a media product – and riches lie in wait. Popular clips include Black20 Trailer Park's PG-rated version, satirising the portentous machismo of the Spartans' shouty dialogue: 'Spartans! Tonight, we dine in *heck*!'. This parody is also a self-parody, sending up the very idea of a PG-rated version of such an unremittingly thuggish R-rated original ('This is delicious!' 'This is *Cake-Town*!'); the authors arm their newly child-friendly Spartan phalanx with candy-canes. The cartoon-like implausibility of these CGI alterations is itself part of the clip's sophisticated humour.

Seen in this new context, the alacrity with which 300's cast and crew spun their film as its own parody ('hysterical weirdness') reads as new-media-savvy damage control – a move to preempt and undercut YouTube's textual poachers. But satire was only half the YouTube story. A search on '300' returns parodies, but also serious news and current-affairs media – from the US, UK and Iran ('Zionist Conspiracy' included) – and numerous self-filmed opinion segments from site members. As with the parodies, these vary widely in sophistication of content and implementation; key '300', and the user takes pot luck. Stakeholders on every side of the critical and political debates around 300 are accessing a huge global audience with an immediacy inconceivable pre-YouTube. The more popular fan clips attract *millions* of viewers – more than most TV shows and many Hollywood films.

By far the most popular parody said it all for many viewers. Suburbania's penetrating critique of 300's hyper-butch politics of masculinity spliced together scenes of rugged male-bonding and set them to an early Eighties disco classic and subsequent gay anthem. The cinema trailers had showcased a stunning, heavily stylised sequence in which the Spartan phalanx bulldozes panicking Persians into the sea from the cliffs at Thermopylae. Now it picked up a new soundtrack:

It's raining men – Hallelujah! It's raining men – Amen!

There was plenty in the 'original' that played, more or less knowingly, to recuperation as camp. The heroic friendship of Stelios and boyish Astinos, a character not in Miller's comic, was a screamingly sublimated gay-romance subplot straight out of *Aeneid* Book 9. They just *so obviously were* Nisus and Euryalus to anyone who'd read Vergil's epic, and their hunkier-than-thou dialogue pushed a heavy subtext of Greek love to everyone who hadn't – from the fanfic writers who'd slashed Brad Pitt's Achilles with absolutely every other male character in *Troy* to the thoroughly mainstream audiences who'd cracked up at *Alexander*'s 'do you love that man?'. *300* didn't just parody itself pre-emptively – in the Stelios/Astinos relationship, it wrote its own slash before anyone else could, knowingly ticking off fanfic clichés to the point of generating its own internal Mary Sue. (A 'Mary Sue' is a classic symptom of self-indulgent relationship fic – the invented character who's transparently the writer's projection of themselves into the canon story.)

'We were all turning gay', Snyder quipped to journalists, selling a narrative he'd otherwise have had to give away. But rewriting *300* as an instant camp classic, inadvertent or otherwise, wasn't the only critique on offer.

OK, so I just got back from the movie *300*, this is gonna be a review. In my opinion, the movie was a butchering of history. Now, there are some spoilers in this review ... I don't want to hear anyone tell me, 'Oh, it's just a movie, it's just fiction ... it's just a comic book, relax, enjoy the entertainment' – no. The show *24* was not 'just entertainment', it was racist, it was demonising Middle Easterners, and the movie 300 was demonising the Persians ... let me go through the points.

This clip, by a Persian-American YouTube regular with the
disarming handle 'persianguyagain', had been viewed nearly 30,000
times at the time of writing and had generated intense debate – 2,000
posted comments and counting. It developed a personal, forceful and
lucid critique of 300's ethnic politics and sheer awkward timing:

> ...they made [the Persian Immortals] look like orcs ... with
> frickin' jutting teeth and face-masks on, okay? In my opinion,
> it's another way to dehumanise the Middle East. I'm just waiting
> for people who are pro-war against Iran to start going 'Oh, *this
> is Sparta*' over and over again after they watch the movie. And
> already people are taking this at face value for historical accu
> racy – I've seen at least fifteen, twenty video tags on YouTube
> of people talking about how 300 is supposedly historically accu
> rate, okay? So this is partly why I'm making the video response
> about it ... basically, the majority of people in this country
> learn geography through wars, and history through Hollywood
> movies like this. That's the problem ... everything about the
> Persian army, they demonised it.

Persianguyagain's followup clip combined a more structured breakdown of the film's failings ('this is a video clarifying that video ... I
hadn't slept for several days and I'd had around four litres of Diet
Coke'); well-argued, pro-Iranian political comment on the release
of the fifteen Brits ... and a 'pretty good' recipe for potato cheese
soup.

Ironically, one audience didn't get to interact and share its point
of view; YouTube was banned in Iran in late 2006.

'Then we will hum in the shade': the Death of the Auteur

> Go tell the Spartans that their sacrifice was not in vain; their
> long day's fight under the cooling shade of a million falling
> arrows safeguarded the West and guaranteed, all these years
> later, the right of idiots to make rotten movies about them.
>
> *Washington Post*

Miller's graphic novel was pre-9/11, pre-Gulf War 2, and apologists
for the film found this convenient. IMDb and YouTube quickly filled
up with naysayers to any and every politicised interpretation. This
was a shot-for-shot remake of a source from a more innocent age,
the argument ran, and a (kids'?) comic at that; critics who read it
as political allegory were doing violence to Miller's and Synder's
intentions.

Miller, of course, had always presented a very clear narrative
about *his* declared intentions and continued to do so in publicity
for the film. But as we saw from the start, 'the film itself' has
always instantly blurred into consumer/fan/critical discourse; its
meanings are constituted by its reception, and the graphic novel
is no different. Auteurist 'intention' lacks its old mystique within
this interpretative frame. With *Troy* and *Alexander*, the Web kicked
this interactivity up a gear; with *300*, streaming video turned the
film into its own instant pastiche. This time, at least, the film in
question had the wit to play along and turn the dynamic to its
commercial advantage. *300* made its money back – and then some
– *in its first weekend* in the US, continued to do brisk trade, and
is cleaning up on DVD – to say nothing of the merchandising. Its
astonishing profitability *might* green-light a new wave of ancient-
world epics; we'll have to wait and see. Certainly the *300* crew are
playing their cards close to the chest when discussing any possible
follow-up. Miller, currently making the apologists' job very difficult

by developing a resolutely agenda-driven 'sock! pow!' Batman-vs.-Al-Qaeda graphic novel – *Holy Terror, Batman!* – insists that 300 is the first of a trilogy of ancient Greek epics, but that his lips are sealed until the studio get their cheque-book out. Synder, previously best known for a solid remake of Romero's *Dawn of the Dead* and always 300's most astute ambassador, has joked that '301' might be a zombie/Spartan crossover: 'Tonight, we dine on *brains*!'.

Actually, dining on brains is what 300 does best – gleefully mindless cannibalism is the key to its workability as a movie and its commercial success. The film gets around the notorious problems of putting Greece on film by taking a leaf from *Xena's* book and whole chapters from everyone else's. Its classical landscape is a deliberately generic composite of visual and soundtrack references, primarily to *Gladiator*. Synder paints an ancient-world-by-numbers, knows it, and knows we know it too – *and* that we know he knows. This heady complicity between film and audience makes for a good time all round. Woman-and-kid in a cornfield? Check. (She even *looks* like Maximus' wife.) Lisa Gerrard sound-alike warbling in the background? Present and correct. Dialogue soundbites? Pretty much word for word ('respect and honour'). And now we can get on with enjoying the pecs and violence.

300's genius, then, is that it's so cheerfully post- and sub-*Gladiator* in a way that the respectability-fixated *Troy* and *Alexander* didn't have the nerve to be. Its real – and very successful – recent forerunners are instead the straight-to-DVD pornographic cash-ins on *Gladiator* whose visual tics it shares. (That waving cornfield is straight out of *Gladiator* ... by way of *Gladiator Eroticus: the Lesbian Warriors*.) At the same time, and opting into *Xena's* cheerful enthusiasms for source-raiding and leather underwear, it brings back to life the scantily-clad Mr Herculeses of the 60s *pepla*: boys, boys, boys. 300 parties on, dude; it knows how to be a properly guilty pleasure, and this makes it the absolute last word on reception of ancient Greece in contemporary mass culture.

For now.

Epilogue

RADIO GAGA

'Is there a Radio *One*?' asked my colleague, in all seriousness. It had never occurred to him before that there might be. A sweet guy, funny, smart (of course), a favourite with the students, he was nobody's idea of a snob. He liked his opera, that was all; he had his own particular habits and ideas about culture and he had honestly never wondered whether there might be something preceding Radios Two, Three and Four. It raised a smile. We all have our blind spots.

'What's the city like for music?' asked the visiting academic, breaking the ice but also genuinely wanting to know.

I started talking about the gigs, the clubs, but the sounds coming out of my mouth were senseless to him; he had asked about *music*. We might as well have been from different planets. A colleague with good timing stepped in and briefed him about the concerts, the orchestras, and he relaxed. I was left feeling like some kind of class dunce. We all know what we mean by 'music' – and 'literature' and 'culture'; but no two meanings agree.

The move from 'culture' to 'popular culture', necessary though I think it is for reception studies, opens up a whole new area of contested meanings. The richness and diversity of contemporary popular culture mean that this book could never be written, or read, the same way twice. From the outset I have pushed an informal personal voice to the front of the narrative; the point I have wanted to stress throughout is not just the impossibility but the undesirability and indeed the *sheer tedious irrelevance* of scholarly 'objectivity' in an enterprise of this kind. We cannot engage critically with popular culture and still (pretend to) keep our hands clean; we need to be clear on where we are coming from, individually and as a subculture (or, if you insist, a 'discipline') – clear in our own heads at least and ideally up front too. This is a challenge that classical studies is still squaring up to, and may well defer indefinitely. The upside of owning up (or one positive spin) is that we can acknowledge and *own* our miscellaneous pet enthusiasms (whether for Great Books or graphic novels), be they ever so irritating – and all in the name of research. Life, for the out-and-proud scholar-fan, is very good indeed; for the cynic, perhaps too good to be true.

Is there a downside? Certainly this kind of criticism carries risk, and not simply in terms of sniffy reviews (and getting personal will mean at least *some* of those; a leaning-towards-caricature version of my blind spots and pet peeves is on open display). One pitfall that cultural studies generally is beginning to take on board is the easy but hollow assumption that 'subcultural' automatically means countercultural – edgy, subversive. Hip academics enjoy talking up 'subversion' of mainstream ideology (as opposed to 'containment') because it sounds cool and is easily theorised; but it's not always there, or not in the form they think it is. (Slash is a particularly good example of a sometimes over-hyped subcultural practice; it is 'subversive', yes, but sometimes more straightforwardly than others.) Classicists are particularly susceptible to this cosy faux-radicalism, in part because of our desire to be relevant but also because we fixate on detail. The danger is that we can end up merely replacing one brand of academic mastery with another. If our professional hitting power is determined by our DVD collection, by the cult comics we've read, the cool authors we've met, or the subcultures we've slept around in, then is that somehow magically 'better' than if it's measured against the number of Great Books we've internalised? We all like to flatter ourselves that we're cutting-edge, but we could easily end up dishing out the same old menu, this time with delusions of hipness and relevance. (Taking no prisoners in his own discipline of Eng. Lit., Richard Burt has named this slippery slope 'Loser Criticism'.) Classicists are the original alpha geeks, and our rush to embrace Film has played to our completist tendency. Widening the picture to take in more explicitly subcultural material is, I've argued, a completely necessary step; but this 'open' and actively participatory model of popular culture sits uneasily with our ingrained professional habits of control and over-specialisation. (Film is far less of a challenge; give us a closed-down canon of trivia and we're happy.) Classics-and-trash was already one step too far for many classicists; classics-and-slash takes us way outside the disciplinary comfort zone. In the meantime, and just by writing about it, a classicist runs the risk of turning into that peren-nial students' nightmare, the trendy don.

But I think it's necessary all the same, regardless of the potential for mortification, and never more so than for receptions of ancient Greece. The Greeks have been made to mean so very much – and in such a narrowly prescribed way, set in stone as the underpinning of all those top-down narratives of the history of ideas and the Western Tradition. We endlessly project these meanings back onto them, like so many flickering and distorted shadows on the wall of the Cave. Historically, these meanings have been narrowly conserva-tive – Culture with an emphatically underlined capital 'C' and no crowd-pleasing concessions. Combine this ideological conservatism with a risk-averse film industry's fixation on formula and it is small wonder that cinema's Greece has replayed Thucydides' ghost-town Sparta scenario. The miracle is that other receptions are creeping in. *Xena* and the rest have proved that Greece *can* be commodified for a mass audience and can turn old myths ('Hercules' and 'Western Tradition' alike) on their heads. We've seen that an ever more diverse and participatory popular culture is leaving the old claims of academic mastery and cultural ownership looking increasingly threadbare. For small-c culture – and subculture, and even counter-culture – the fun with the ancient Greeks is just beginning. Here, too, Thucydides remains good to think with. His complaint was that Greece's intractably fiddly terrain made joined-up, top-down history a thankless uphill struggle, but he might just as easily have been talking about Greece *in reception* – where all the fun and profit is in bottom-up narratives, diversity, up-front subjectivity (in every applicable sense). Significantly, though, these new receptions *aren't* happening in film – or weren't until 300. It'll be intriguing to see how or if anyone manages to follow that.

Reception will continue to have its ups and downs, but it still holds out to classical studies the promise of a genuinely different way of doing things. Not just 'classics and film', nor even 'classics and popular culture': everything we do, absolutely everything, is reception. The challenge now is: do we face up to that, and even, perish the thought, have some fun of our own? For whether we classicists like the idea or not, the promise that reception holds out to a wider culture is one that's already coming true, all the time, and 'objectivity' be damned: new ancient worlds for old.

GLOSSARY

180° rule. A basic rule of **cinematography**, establishing continuity when filming an exchange between characters, is to keep one of them 'stage left' and the other 'stage right'. Film-makers often think in terms of an invisible line drawn between the two characters and extending beyond them. The director can set up close-up shots from any angle he or she likes, provided that the camera stays on one side of that invisible line – that is, within a 180° arc. Otherwise, the characters appear to 'swap places'. The line can only be crossed by physically moving the camera across it while filming – a tracking shot.

Auteur, Auteurism. The figure of the 'auteur' characterises the film director as artist, expressing a personal vision, like a painter or a novelist. 'Auteurism' is a style of film criticism that emphasises the role of the director as an independent creator who determines the film's meaning; it plays down both the collaborative, industrialised film-making process and the audience's active role in negotiating meaning. Expressed in reviews and popular writing on film, it turns individual directors into cult figures with **star image** and establishes a pecking order or canon of 'great directors'. Although this is something I'm concerned to avoid, parts of ch.1 in particular skirt the edges of auteurist criticism.

Blogger. A private individual who makes their journal available online as a weblog or 'blog'.

Camp. Diluted by mainstream culture to mean little more than 'kitsch', 'camp' originally characterised gay men's **subcultural** readings of mainstream, non-gay media material. At a time when little material addressed gay men directly, camp enabled the fledgling gay scene to improvise a 'canon' of borrowed media products (particularly films and TV shows) which gave the scene a shared aesthetic. **Star image** was often crucial to the appropriation of this material; gay men explored their own identities as outsiders via an ironic identification which was playful but also emotionally resonant. Judy Garland films are a much-cited example. Recruited for camp viewing, Garland 'acted out' – and served as a model for – the emotional lives of her gay male audiences, and inspired countless drag acts. As gay identities achieve mainstream visibility, 'camp' is becoming gradually sidelined by the more explicit and oppositional 'queer'.

Cinematography. What the film-makers do with the camera. Pans and zooms; setting up a tracking shot via a wheeled 'dolly'; choosing between a long shot to establish or re-establish a setting, or a head-and-shoulders close-up to get our attention on the star; selecting a high or a low camera angle: these are all cinematography. Cinematography and **mise-en-scène** are useful terms, but the distinction between them tends to blur in practice. Film-makers' decisions about lighting and colour (mise-en-scène), for instance, will invariably be influenced by their choices concerning film stock (cinematography).

Erastes and **eromenos**. To over-generalise, but only slightly: the ancient world had no concept of 'homosexuality' as an inherent sexual orientation, or, for that matter, of 'heterosexuality'. Similarly, Greeks and Romans lacked the idea of 'sin' that we get from the monotheistic religions, and it did not occur to them to feel guilty for experiencing sexual desire. But they had a strong sense of public shame which led them to develop more or less rigid codes of tasteful sexual behaviour. Instead of degrees of sinfulness, distinctions of status – of gender, class, and age – were the concerns that determined how sexual relations played out. One partner was always unambiguously 'on top' and the power imbalance would usually be acted out via penetration. The Greek and particularly Athenian ideal for same-sex relationships between free men was a relationship between an older, active lover, the **erastes**, and a youthful, passive beloved, the **eromenos**. It was the responsibility of the *erastes* to woo the *eromenos* with gifts, give him the benefit of his hard-won experience and induct him into the manly virtues. The *eromenos*, in turn, was supposed to resist the advances of the *erastes* at first (so as not to incur shame by being too 'easy') and then to submit to his sexual needs. As the inferior – albeit desired – partner, his own sexual pleasure was not important. The *erastes-eromenos* relationship, as idealised in (for instance) Plato's *Symposium*, resembles later ideals of chivalric and romantic love. At the same time, it was meant to be a phase, particularly for the *eromenos*. It would be shameful for him to continue to submit sexually as a mature adult – that is, once he had the equal status that went with being a full citizen. The good taste of the *erastes* would be called into question, too, if he expressed a preference for a man who no longer matched the aesthetic ideal of beardless youth; people could no longer be sure that he was the active partner.

Fandom. Generic term for the various and inter-related **subcultures** of fan activity associated with science fiction, fantasy, comics, role-playing games and other minority cultural products. 'Fandom' implies a quasi-tribal sense of community, a sense reinforced by participatory cultural forms (e.g. **slash**) and a regular circuit of conventions ('cons') run by and for fans, by fan publications ('zines'), and latterly via websites and newsgroups. Fans consider themselves to be members of distinctive subcultures which set them apart from the mainstream culture of non-fans ('mundanes').

Hellenistic. By convention, the 'Hellenistic Age' begins with the death of Alexander the Great (323 BC), when his vast empire dissolved into rival kingdoms ruled by his former generals. It ends with the death of Cleopatra (31 BC), the last ruler of the last of these kingdoms to fall to Rome.

Mise-en-scène. What the film-makers put in front of the camera (literally, what is 'put on the stage'). Sets and props, costuming, lighting effects: these are all mise-en-scène. The actors' performances, too, are often counted as part of the mise-en-scène.

Montage. Pioneered by Soviet film-maker Sergei Eisenstein, montage is a sequence of thematically varied and often stylised shots edited together into a sequence from which a meaning emerges. Eisenstein intended montage to be a vehicle for Marxist dialectic but it was quickly appropriated by capitalist Hollywood. Montage is often used to convey a process of change over time; the movie audience join the dots, filling in the 'story' between the shots.

Other, The. Overexposed but still useful concept from Structuralist cultural criticism. Within any society, the majority tends to objectify outsiders and marginalized groups (e.g. women, gays, immigrants, the unemployed) as 'Other', rather than engaging with them in their diversity as individuals. This 'Other' is a fantasy projected by the mainstream onto foreigners, minorities and underdogs, embodying all the characteristics the majority would prefer not to associate with itself (laziness, poor hygiene, emotional instability, non-approved sexual acts, etc). The majority uses the Other to define itself by what it is not – or by what it would like to think it is not.

Peplum (plural: **pepla**). A term used to characterise films set in ancient Greece, often dismissively. Roman movies are sometimes called 'toga films', after the wrap-around robe worn by male Roman citizens; so calling these films *pepla* ('cloaks') implicitly sets them up as cheap toga knock-offs. Actually the *peplum* isn't a particularly close equivalent to the Roman toga – it's a women's cloak. The closest match would be the Greek *himation* or *chlamys*, but *peplum* is much easier to pronounce.

Reception. The study of ways in which a culture's ideas about the past – e.g., classical antiquity – are formed and of how these ideas are put to work in the present. An unambiguous twentieth-century example would be Mussolini's use of Augustan Rome to generate visual imagery for modern Italian Fascism, and to justify its territorial ambitions. Film's visions of the past have tended to serve modern concerns, too. Maria Wyke (*Projecting the Past*) has shown how Hollywood's Cold War narratives of early Christians versus pagans in ancient Rome are filled with coded references to the films' contemporary political contexts: wholesome American values score physical and moral victories over totalitarian emperors who resemble Hitler and Stalin. More broadly, Simon Goldhill (*Who Needs Greek?*) has explored the turbulent afterlife of Greek and Greekness in Western culture from the Renaissance to the Victorians. Unavoidably, the academic disciplines of classics, archaeology and ancient history are also receptions of the ancient world; the best we can hope for is to make them self-conscious and interestingly complicated ones. See: **Further Reading**.

Star image. As articulated by film theorist Richard Dyer (*Stars*), 'star image' describes the baggage – mannerisms, characterisations, gossip – that star actors bring with them to particular film performances. 'Stars' are neither flesh-and-blood people nor film characters but fetishised commodities that blur the divide between reality and fiction. Star image can be personally empowering (audiences develop identifications with particular stars: see also **camp**); it is also a powerful and versatile marketing tool. 'Arnie' is a particularly useful contemporary example, combining the body beautiful, politics, fast-food commerce and self-pastiche. Jackie Stacey (*Star Gazing*) offers a particularly useful account of female audiences' escapist and aspirational engagements with female stars in the 1940s and 50s. See: **Further Reading**.

Slash fiction. Unauthorised fiction, written by and for fans, which imaginatively fleshes out the personalities and personal lives of characters from popular science fiction and fantasy TV series (e.g. *Buffy*, *Xena*). Slash fiction circulates primarily within **fandom** via **subcultural** forms including zines and, now, the internet. Strictly defined, slash is erotic – and, particularly, homoerotic – in its scenarios. The original slash fiction was written by female fans of the original *Star Trek* series; it postulated sexual encounters between Captain Kirk and his Vulcan science officer Spock, with a level of detail that ranged from sub-Mills and Boon romance to hardcore porn, and explored the odd couple's developing romantic relationship. This sub-genre of fan fiction became known as 'Kirk / Spock', or 'K / S'; in discussions of the form, the slash mark was vocalised ('K-slash-S'). When fans started writing similar fiction about other characters, the name 'slash' stuck.

Subculture. The academic discipline of cultural studies uses 'culture' in a broad sense, to mean the whole body of activities and products that transmit and create a society's shared meanings. 'Culture' is not just the High Culture of art and literature, but also journalism, TV shows, fashion and design, popular music, advertising, fast food, graffiti – the list could go on and on. The term 'subculture' is used to describe groups within the larger culture that claim an identity distinct from (or even opposed to) the mainstream. Academic studies have concentrated on music subcultures such as punk; subcultures of **fandom** based around genre and 'cult' media, including science fiction and comics; and sexual subcultures, such as the gay, lesbian and SM 'scenes'. Members express and create their subcultural identities via shared cultural forms (often subsequently appropriated by the mainstream): the way they dress, the books and music they argue about, the clubs they attend, the slang they use.

Suggestions for Further Reading (and Viewing)

L ike the rest of the *Greece and Rome Live!* series, this book was written with the interested general reader in mind as well as students and scholars in the field. Non-classicists may be shocked to discover how expensive books can be in a specialist field like classical studies. I've tried to give a rough indication of likely costs for readers wishing to pursue particular topics further. Books marked with an asterisk (*) are available in paperback at relatively affordable prices, generally £12 – £16 or so and sometimes less. After that, prices rise steeply.

The section ends with a selective Filmography. I've been at pains to avoid underwriting a 'canon' for the *pepla*, but these are the films that most fans would agree would be in it – the must-sees.

General: Classical Studies

*Mary Beard and John Henderson, *Classics: A Very Short Introduction* (Oxford University Press, 1995).
    —Fine, punchy and provocative introduction to the questions and issues that make classical studies important, by two of the most interesting classicists out there.

*Simon Goldhill, *Love, Sex and Tragedy: Why Classics Matters* (John Murray, 2005).

—Entertainingly partial thematic introduction to ancient culture and its long reach into the modern collective unconscious. Heavily Greek-biased, so a useful read to broaden the context; and strikingly conservative in its (strongly felt) assumptions about which bits of culture matter, so an interesting contrast.

General: Film and TV Studies

*John Hill and Pamela Church Gibson, *Film Studies: Critical Approaches* (Oxford University Press, 2000).
—Handy, affordable collection of introductory essays. The expert contributors cover all the key areas of film studies concisely and accessibly.

*Mark Jancovich (ed.), *Quality Popular Television: Cult TV, the Industry and Fans* (University of Exeter Press, 2003).
—Usefully diverse collection of essays, including some *Xena* material; makes a nice follow-up read to Jenkins.

*Henry Jenkins, *Textual Poachers* (Routledge, 1992).
—Fun, frank and nicely thought through, *Textual Poachers* was ground-breaking at the time and has still not been bettered as an account of how fans use and rework media texts within subcultures. His more recent work on 'convergence culture' is also well worth your time.

*Tom Shone, *Blockbuster: How Hollywood Learned to Stop Worrying and Love the Summer* (Simon & Schuster, 1994).
—Funny and persuasive account of the rise of the big dumb movie; shows you why particular projects end up the way they do.

General: Romans and Greeks on Film

*Monica Silveira Cyrino, *Big Screen Rome* (Blackwell, 2005)
—Peky, covers lots of bases for teaching.

*Sandra M. Joshel, Margaret Malamud and Donald T. McGuire, Jr.
(eds), *Imperial Projections: Ancient Rome in Modern Popular Culture*
(Johns Hopkins, 2001).
—Worthwhile if limited supplement to Wyke's *Projecting the
Past*, broadening the field of enquiry to include Roman-themed
comedies and TV drama (*I, Claudius*) and the Caesars Palace
casino in Las Vegas. The jacket sells *Imperial Projections* on the
back of *Gladiator* (2000), but the book itself rarely gets more
'modern' than the mid-1960s, and its range is less diverse than
the sales pitch would lead you to expect.

*Arthur J. Pomeroy, *Then it was Destroyed by the Volcano: The Ancient
World in Film and on Television* (Duckworth, 2008)
—Light in methodology, broad in coverage, with useful material
on non-Western receptions. Don't be put off by the cover

*Jon Solomon, *The Ancient World in the Cinema: revised and expanded
edition* (Yale University Press, 2001).
—Chatty, engaging and endlessly digressive, this is a mine of
information – and a bargain in paperback. Factually very accu-
rate on the whole, it's more concerned to present the material
entertainingly than to pick it apart via analysis. Includes a
hugely enjoyable chapter on the Italian muscleman films.

*Maria Wyke, *Projecting the Past: Ancient Rome, Cinema and History* (Routledge, 1997).
—Cinema as alternative historiography, trash as 'classics': this influential book develops a series of case studies in the representation of ancient Rome by Italian and Hollywood film-makers. Thoughtful and affordable, *Projecting the Past* is a staple of undergraduate 'classics in film' courses and a must-have for anyone wishing to pursue the subject further.

General: Receptions of Classical Antiquity

Catharine Edwards (ed.), *Roman Presences: Receptions of Rome in European Culture, 1789–1945* (Cambridge University Press, 1999).
—Intelligent, adventurous collection of essays on the centrality of Rome to the European imagination from Napoleon to the Nazis. Alas, expensive even in paperback.

*Simon Goldhill, *Who Needs Greek? Contests in the Cultural History of Hellenism* (Cambridge University Press, 2002).
—Thought-provoking assemblage of case studies in Western ambivalence towards Greek and the idea of Greece, from the Renaissance to the Victorian era. Affordable in paperback, but the same author's *Love, Sex and Tragedy* covers many of the same topics more approachably and for less money.

*Lorna Hardwick, *Greece and Rome New Surveys in the Classics no.33: Reception Studies* (Oxford University Press, 2003).
—A little dry, and inclined towards Classical Tradition mainstays (theatre and poetry), but good value at well under a tenner.

Lorna Hardwick and Christopher Stray (eds), *A Companion to Classical Receptions* (Blackwell, 2008)
—Good, big and cripplingly expensive.

Richard Jenkyns, *The Victorians and Ancient Greece* (Blackwell, 1980).
—Very old-fashioned (knee-jerk elitism, now-offensive ideas about sexuality) but, in an old-fashioned way, crammed full of delightful scraps of gossipy connoisseurship.

Charles Martindale and Richard Thomas (eds), *Classics and the Uses of Reception* (Blackwell 2006)
—A thoughtful new collection of essays with some lively contributors and a welcome emphasis on how we theorise 'reception'.

Chapter One: Socrates' Excellent Adventure

*Alastair Blanshard, *Hercules: A Heroic Life* (Granta, 2005).
—Lots of fun, and includes a chapter on the *pepla*.

*Catharine Edwards, *Writing Rome: Textual Approaches to the City* (Cambridge University Press, 1996).
—Excellent short book on how Rome turned itself into an urban legend in its own lifetime.

Ed Naha, *The Films of Roger Corman: Brilliance on a Budget* (Simon and Schuster, 1990).
—Critical study of Corman's colossal output.

*Frank Thompson, *Lost Films: Important Movies That Disappeared* (Citadel, 1996).
—My principal source on the lost 1917 *Cleopatra*. Currently out of print.

*Martin Winkler (ed.), *Troy: From Homer's Iliad to Hollywood Epic* (Blackwell, 2007).
—Nicely produced but pretty basic.

Chapter Two: Mythconceptions

Maria Wyke, 'Herculean Muscle! The classicizing rhetoric of body-building', *Arion* 4.3 (1997).

*Maria Wyke, *Projecting the Past: Ancient Rome, Cinema and History* (Routledge, 1997).
—My discussion of the Italian version of *Quo Vadis?* leans heavily on Chapter 5 of Maria's influential book.

Paul Zanker, *The Power of Images in the Age of Augustus* (University of Michigan Press, 1988).
—Includes an eye-opening analysis of Antony and Octavian's image war.

Premiere magazine (September 2004 edition).
—Lots of *Troy* goodies. Libby Gelman-Waxner's article 'Queer Eye for the Greek Guy' is my obvious source for subtext-riffling critique of 'Homer-erotic' *Troy*.

Chapter Three: Wars of the Successors

*Richard Dyer, *Stars* (British Film Institute, 1979).
   —Influential, well-written book on star image.

*Diana Spencer, *The Roman Alexander: Reading a Cultural Myth* (Exeter University Press, 2002).
   —Thought-provoking account of 'Alexander' as a name to conjure with, from antiquity to the present. The main emphasis is on Roman receptions of Alexander's myth, but there's more recent material too. A very refreshing change from the usual nitpicking over 'the real Alexander'.

*Jackie Stacey, *Star Gazing: Hollywood Cinema and Female Spectatorship* (Routledge, 1994).
   —Moves on nicely from Dyer (1979) and is particularly good on female audiences.

*Martin Winkler (ed.), *Gladiator: Film and History* (Blackwell, 2004).
   —Includes Kathleen Coleman's coldly furious reflections on *Gladiator*'s misuse of her expertise.

*Michael Wood, *In the Footsteps of Alexander the Great* (BBC Consumer Publishing, 2001)
   —The epic, continent-spanning saga of one man's obsessive quest for immortality – and that's just the author. Actually, the book (spun off from the 1997 TV series, and priced to sell) is packed with interesting material. Wood is particularly useful on non-Western receptions of Alexander.

Web Resources

URLs were correct at the time of going to press.

http://www2.open.ac.uk/ClassicalStudies/GreekPlays/crsn/index.
shtml
—The Classical Reception Studies Network; organises frequent
academic workshops and conferences.

www.imdb.com
—The Internet Movie Database. Comprehensive, user-friendly
and indispensable, IMDb has rendered whole genres of film book
obsolete overnight.

www.isidore-of-seville.com, www.pothos.org
—useful, intelligent Alexander fan sites.

www.briansdriveintheater.com/
—Excellent Hercules film fan site; informative and well
illustrated.

www.ugo.com/channels/filmtv/features/williamshatner/
—My source for the William Shatner interview quoted in ch.3.

www.gayheroes.com/
—A long-established gay and lesbian history site which gives
star billing to Alexander in its upbeat survey of famous gay
historical figures.

www.sun.rhbnc.ac.uk/Classics/NJL/novels.html
—Nick Lowe's 'Ancient Greece in Fiction'.

www.whoosh.org
—Homepage of the International Association of Xena Studies,
online since 1996. No longer active, but a large archive of useful
and fun resources. 'Whoosh!' is the noise Xena's chakram makes
as it flies through the air.

Filmography

The last thing I want to do is peddle another ersatz canon, but a
notional top ten, chronologically arranged, might look a bit like this:

Ulysses (1955)
(alternate title: *Ulisse*)
Dir. Mario Camerini, Mario Bava
Lux Film

Helen of Troy (1956)
Dir. Robert Wise
Warner Bros

Alexander the Great (1956)
Dir. Robert Rossen
C.B. Films / Rossen Films

Hercules (1958)
(alternate title: *Le Fatiche di Ercole*)
Dir. Pietro Francisci
Embassy Pictures (dubbed version) / Galatea Film / O.S.C.A.R./
Urania Film

Jason and the Argonauts (1963)
(alternate title: *Jason and the Golden Fleece*)
Dir. Don Chaffey
Columbia Pictures / Morningside Worldwide

Clash of the Titans (1981)
Dir. Desmond Davis
MGM / Titan Productions

Hercules (1997)
Dir. Ron Clements / John Musker
Walt Disney Pictures

Troy (2004)
Dir. Wolfgang Petersen
Warner Bros / Radiant / Plan B

Alexander (2004)
Dir. Oliver Stone
Warner Bros / Intermedia / Pacifica / Egmond / IMF

And, in at number one – with a bullet,

300 (2006)
Dir. Zach Snyder
Warner Bros / Legendary Pictures

INDEX